Wood Pellet Smoker and Grill Cookbook

Delicious and Easy BBQ Recipes to make you a Grilling Master

Mark Spencer

Table of Contents

What Is a Wood Pellet Smoker and Grill?

This piece of equipment is a cooker which burns wood. You can use it to bake, smoke, or grill meat. A pellet smoker and grill is fueled using wood pellets. These pellets burn slowly and do not leave too much dust behind. A wood pellet is made of compressed, food-grade wood, which burns at a lower temperature when compared to other wood chips. These smokers are great if you want to cook a rack of ribs, fish, turkey, brisket, and more. They give the meat a smoky flavor. It is easy to work with wood pellet smokers. All you must do is open the lid to flip the meat, use a marinade to dress the meat, and rotate the meat in the grill section of the equipment.

You can choose from various models. If you are new to using a wood pellet smoker or grill, base your selection on the following parameters:

- Cooking area
- Warming rack size
- Temperature control options
- Digital controllers and other accouterments

Most wood pellet smokers have a stainless-steel interior, but if you are a traditionalist, you can use a cast-iron model. Since there are so many models in the market, it is important to find the model which works best for you. Now that you know what a pellet smoker is, let us look at how one works.

How Does a Pellet Smoker Work?

The fire or burn pot in the pellet smoker is present at the bottom of the pellet smoker or grill. This is the cooking chamber where you burn the hardwood and charcoal pellets. The heat from the cooking chamber circulates through the convection, thereby cooking the meat. You need to lay the meat on the cooking grill and turn it to ensure the meat is fully cooked through.

The advantage with using a pellet smoker is you do not have to struggle with adding more wood to cook the meat. The pellets are present above the cooking chamber in a pellet hopper. When the wood pellets in the chamber are fully burnt, the pellet hopper pushes more pellets into the chamber through a chute.

The airflow in the pellet smoker controls the temperature at which the meat is cooked. If you want to increase the temperature, you only need to turn the heavy-duty fans on. These fans are located at the bottom of the cooking chamber, and they suck the air from the heart of the chamber to the bottom. This allows the heat to leave the smoker when you open the lid.

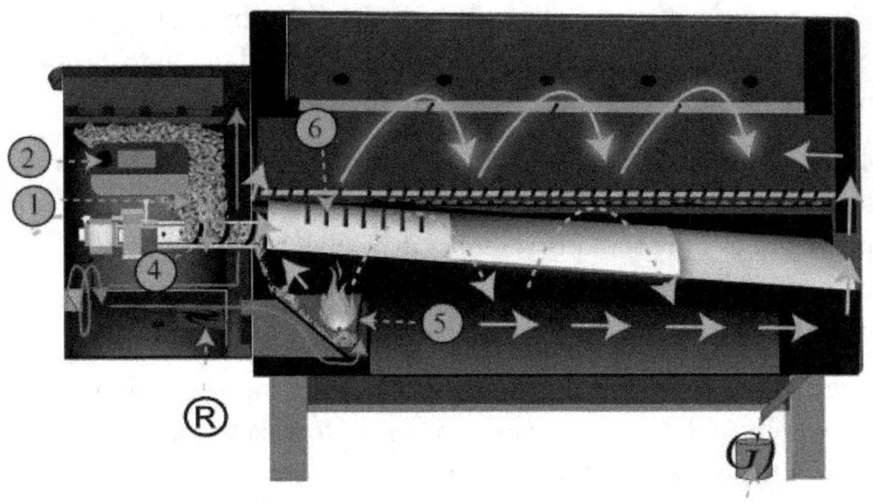

CD Hardwood Pellets
are loaded into the Hopper

,:::;\ The Controller regulates
\!::.J temperature automatically

a\ The Induction Fan stokes
\V theflre

© The Auger carries the Pellets
to the Firepot

(D The Hot Rod ignites the Pellets

/'Z\ Heat & smoke circuiate through
the Barre l

,;;\ The Drip Tray keeps grease away
\!...J from the flre

Poultry

BBQ Halved Chickens

Prep Time: 15 Minutes

Cook Time: 1 Hour

Serving: 8 people

Ingredients

- (5 Lb.) Chicken
- 1/3 Cup of Honey
- 2 Cups Water
- Tablespoon Oil
- 1/4 Cup of Traeger Pork and Poultry Rub
- 1/3 Cup Traeger 'Que BBQ Sauce
- 1/3 Cup Traeger Apricot BBQ Sauce
- 6 Tablespoon of Butcher BBQ Bird Booster in Honey Flavor
- 1 Tablespoon of Apple Cider Vinegar

Instructions

1. Place the chicken on a chopping board, breast-side down, with the neck facing away from the face.

2. From the neck to tail, cut down one side of the backbone, keeping as near the bone as possible. Duplicate on the other half of the backbone, then take it out.

3. Slice through the white cartilage just at the tip of the chicken's breastbone to burst it open. Cut along each side of the breast bone, then pull it out with the fingers.

4. To make Butcher BBQ Bird Booster, combine 2 cups of water

and the Butcher BBQ Bird Booster. Allow at least 30 mins for the injection to settle before straining it via a fine mesh filter.

5. One full tube should be injected into the leg, another into the thigh, & two into the breast. Place the skin-side of the chicken up on a sheet tray & refrigerate for 3 hours, uncovered.

6. Apply canola oil to the skin and generously season with Traeger Pork and Poultry Rub.

7. When ready to cook, preheat the Traeger to 325°F for 15 minutes with the lid closed.

8. Cook for 1 to 1-1/2 hrs. Or until the internal temperature reaches 160°F, directly on the grill grate, skin-side up.

9. Combine the Traeger 'Que BBQ & Apricot BBQ Sauce, Honey, & vinegar in a mixing bowl. Cook for another 5 minutes after brushing the sauce all over the skin of the chicken.

10. Remove off the grill & set aside to rest for 5 minutes before slicing. Enjoy.

Smoked Cajun Chicken Wings

Prep Time: 5 Minutes

Cook Time: 1 Hour

Serves: 6 people

Ingredients

- 1/4 Cup Butter
- 1/4 Teaspoon Salt
- 1 Tablespoon Baking Powder
- 1 Tablespoon of Worcestershire Sauce
- 1/8 Teaspoon Cayenne Pepper
- 1/2 Teaspoon of Dried Thyme
- 1 teaspoon of Paprika
- 1/2 Teaspoon of Garlic Powder
- 1/2 Teaspoon of Onion Powder
- 1/4 Teaspoon Cumin
- 1/4 Teaspoon Freshly Ground Black Pepper
- 3 Pound Chicken Wings, Flats & Drumettes Separated
- 1/4 Cup of Louisiana-Style Hot Sauce
- 1/4 Teaspoon of Dried Oregano

Instructions

1. Rub: Combine baking powder, garlic powder, paprika, onion powder, cumin, thyme, oregano, salt, pepper, & cayenne in a small bowl.

2. Clean the chicken wings by rinsing them and patting them dry with paper towels. Toss the wings in a large mixing basin with

the rub to evenly coat them.

3. Inside an aluminium foil-lined baking sheet, place a wire rack. Arrange the wings in a single layer, leaving a little gap between them. Refrigerate the baking sheet with the wings for eight hours to overnight.

4. Set the temperature to 180°F and preheat for 15 minutes with the lid covered when ready to cook.

5. For 30 minutes, smoke the wings.

6. Raise the temperature of the grill to 350°F after 30 minutes & roast for 40 - 50 mins.

7. Mix butter, hot sauce, & Worcestershire sauce while the wings are on the grill. Bring to a low simmer over medium heat & stir until everything is well mixed.

8. Reduce to a low heat setting & keep warm till the wings are done.

9. Place the wings in a large mixing basin. Toss in the sauce to coat the wings completely.

10. Serve immediately with carrot & blue cheese, celery sticks, ranch, or preferred dipping sauces on a plate. Enjoy!

Smoky Fried Chicken

Prep Time: 10 Minutes

Cook Time: 3 Hours

Serves: 6 people

Ingredients

- 2 Whole Chickens
- Some Vegetable Oil
- Kosher Salt & Black Pepper
- 1 Quart Buttermilk
- 2 Tablespoon of Crystal Hot Sauce
- 2 Tablespoon of Garlic Powder
- 1 Tablespoon of Poultry Rub
- 2 cups of Flour
- 1 Tablespoon of Dark Brown
- Sugar Oil, For Frying
- 2 Tablespoon of Kosher Salt
- 2 Tablespoon of Onion
- Powder Freshly Grounded Black Pepper

Instructions

1. Set the Traeger to almost 200°F and warm for 10 minutes with the lid covered when you're ready to cook. If Super Smoke is available, use it for the best taste.

2. Wash the chickens well under water, both inside and out. Pat dry. Position on a baking sheet with a rim.

3. Season the outsides of all birds with black pepper and salt after

rubbing them with vegetable oil. Arrange the birds straight on the grill plate & smoke for two and a half hrs. Or till the thermometer shows 150°F in the thigh's thickest parts.

4. Allow the smoked chickens to chill on the baking sheet.

5. Four drumsticks, thighs, and wings each, & 8 breast sections - chop the birds into 10 pieces

6. Separate the chicken into two sealed bags.

7. Meanwhile, mix the buttermilk, hot sauce, & brown sugar in a large mixing basin till the crystals of sugar dissolve.

8. Pour half of the mixture into the chicken bag. Refrigerate for an hour after sealing.

9. Whisk together the flour, Garlic & onion powder, seasoning (poultry), and two kosher pepper and salt teaspoons in a separate bowl. Place aside.

10. In an oven of Dutch, heavy saucepan, or deep cast-iron skillet, heat 2" of oil to 375°F over medium-high heat.

11. Drain the pieces of chicken. Dredge each one in the flour mix one at a time.

12. Grill the chicken in the stages until golden brown, approximately six mins for the other pieces & eight mins for the thighs, the wings, & drumsticks, flipping as required with tongs.

13. Before serving, drain using paper towels. Enjoy!

Chipotle Honey Wings

Prep Time: 5 Minutes

Cook Time: 30 Minutes

Serves: 4 people

Ingredients

- 3 Can (7 Oz) of Chipotle Peppers in Adobo Sauce
- 1 Tablespoon of Honey
- 2 Tablespoon Lime Juice
- Avocado Crema, Ranch / Blue Cheese Dressing, For Serving
- 2 Pound Chicken Wings, Flats & Drumettes Separated Traeger Blackened Saskatchewan Rub
- Traeger Chicken Rub
- 4 Tablespoon of Unsalted Butter Lime Wedges, For Garnishing

Instructions

1. Set the Traeger to 350°F & preheat for 15 minutes with the lid covered when you're ready to cook.

2. Season the chicken flats & drumettes lightly on both halves with a mixture of Traeger Chicken Rub & Blackened Saskatchewan Rub on a baking sheet.

3. Cook the chicken wings for 30 minutes on the grill grate.

4. In the meanwhile, melt the butter with the chipotles in a skillet over low heat. Puree the Ingredients in a blender or with an immersion blender once the butter has melted. Combine the honey & lime juice in a mixing bowl. (To taste, add additional honey or lime.)

5. Transfer the wings to a bowl and mix with the honey-lime glaze (chipotle) after they've finished cooking. Serve with

ranch, avocado crema, or blue cheese dressing, & lime wedges
on the side. Enjoy!

Sweet Cajun Wings

Prep Time: 5 Minutes

Cook Time: 30 Minutes

Serves: 4 people

Ingredients

- Traeger Pork and Poultry Rub
- 2 Pound Chicken Wings Traeger Cajun Shake

Instructions

1. Traeger Sweet Rub and Cajun Shake are used to coat the wings.
2. Preheat the Traeger to 350°F for 15 minutes with the lid closed when ready to cook.
3. Cook for half an hour, or till the skin is brown & the interior is juicy, & an instant-read thermometer registers at least 165 degrees F. Serve and enjoy!

Whole Smoked Chicken

Prep Time: 10 Minutes

Cook Time: 3 Hours

Serves: 6 people

Ingredients

Brine

- 1 (3 To 3-1/2 Lb.) Whole Chicken
- 1/2 Cup of Kosher Salt
- 1 Cup of Brown Sugar Traeger Chicken Rub
- 1 Teaspoon of Minced Garlic
- 1 Yellow Onion, Quartered
- 3 Garlic Cloves
- 5 Thyme Sprigs
- 1 Lemon, Halved

Instructions

1. In 1 gallon of water, dissolve the kosher salt & brown sugar. Put the chicken in brine & refrigerate overnight after the salt has dissolved. Make sure the bird is completely immersed, and if necessary, weigh it down.

2. When ready to cook, preheat the Traeger to 225°F with the lid closed for about 15 minutes. If Super Smoke is available, use it for the best taste.

3. Retrieve the chicken from brine & pat dry while the grill warms up. Combine the minced Garlic & Traeger Chicken Rub in a mixing bowl. Fill the interior with lemon, Garlic, Garlic, onion, & thyme. Join the legs by tying them together.

4. Place the chicken on the grill grate & smoke for 2 1/2 to 3

hours, or until a thermometer inserted in the thickest portion of the breast registers 160°F. As the bird rests, the internal temperature of the breast will increase to 165°F. Allow 15 minutes for resting before slicing. Enjoy!

Roast Chicken & Pimento Potatoes

Prep Time: 15 Minutes

Cook Time: 1 Hour

Serves: 8 people

Ingredients

- 6 Tablespoons of Extra-Virgin Olive Oil

- 2 Whole Chickens

- 3 Tablespoons of Pimento (Spanish Smoked Paprika)

- 6 Clove of Garlic, Chopped

- 2 Tablespoons of Salt Salt

- 2 Bunch of Thyme

- 3 Pound Yukon Gold Potatoes

- 1/2 Cup of Chopped Flat-Leaf Parsley

- Ground Black Pepper

- 2 Lemons, Halved

Instructions

1. Remove any giblets and rinse the birds well under cold running water, both inside and out. Using paper towels, thoroughly dry. Tuck the wings under the backs and tie the legs together using butcher's string.

2. To make the spice paste, whisk together the Garlic, salt, & pimento in a small basin. 3 tbsp. extra virgin olive oil. Using your hands, smear the paste all over the birds' outsides. Place one bunch of thyme into each bird's primary cavity. Refrigerate it for at least 6 hours (uncovered) or overnight, on a baking sheet with a rim.

3. Season the scrubbed potatoes with pepper and salt in a large mixing basin. Drizzle the remaining 3 tbsp. Of oil over the vegetables and toss to coat. In a large grill pan or on a wide-rimmed baking sheet, spread out the potatoes.

4. Arrange the chickens on the top of potatoes in a line. Squeeze lemons over the birds & toss the rinds in with the potatoes.

5. Start the Traeger & adjust the temperature to 400 to 450F when you're ready to cook (205-230 C). Preheat for 10 - 15 mins with the lid closed.

6. For 30 minutes, roast the birds, potatoes, & lemons. Toss the potatoes together. Reduce the heat to 350°F (175°C) & continue to roast for another 40 minutes, or until a thermometer placed in the thickest part of thighs reads 165°F (75°C).

7. On a wide plate, arrange the potatoes & lemons. Garnish with parsley and a thin dusting of pimento. Place the chickens on top of it. Enjoy!

Dry Brine Traeger Turkey

Prep Time: 5 Minutes

Cook Time: 6 Hours

Serves: 6 people

Ingredients

- Fresh Sage Fresh Rosemary
- 1 Teaspoon of Kosher Salt Per Pound of Turkey
- Fresh Thyme Fresh Parsley
- 1 Farm Fresh Turkey

Instructions

1. With kosher salt, combine appropriate quantities of thyme, sage, rosemary, and parsley. Rub the kosher salt & spice mixture all over the turkey, including into the cavity.

2. Seal the turkey tightly in a bag / plastic wrap. Refrigerate the turkey for two days. On the third day, remove the turkey from the bag or untie the plastic wrap. Return the turkey to the fridge, uncovered, for another 24 hours.

3. Set the Traeger to 180°F & preheat for 15 minutes with the lid covered when you're ready to cook.

4. Place the turkey breast side up on the grill. Cook the turkey for about 3 - 4 hours on the grill.

5. Increase the grill temperature to 325°F after 3 - 4 hours & continue to cook the turkey till it reaches an interior temperature of 165°F. Enjoy!

BBQ Chicken Wings 3 Ways

Prep Time: 10 Minutes

Cook Time: 35 Minutes

Serves: 4 people

Ingredients

- Chicken Wings
- 8 Pound Chicken Wings Salt
- 1/4 Cup of Spicy Brown Mustard
- 2 Tablespoons of Cornstarch Franks Red-hot Sauce
- 1/2 Cup of Frank's Red-hot Sauce
- 6 Ounce Traeger Chicken Rub
- 6 Tablespoons of Unsalted Butter Sriracha Wing Sauce
- 1/2 Cup of Honey
- 1/2 Cup of Sriracha
- 2 Tablespoons of Sesame Oil
- 1/4 Cup of Soy Sauce

Instructions

1. Preheat oven to 375°F with the lid closed for fifteen minutes when ready to cook.

2. Dry the wings of the chicken with a paper towel while the grill is heating up. In a large mixing bowl, combine the wings, cornstarch, Traeger Chicken Rub, & salt to taste. Coat both halves of the chicken wings with the mixture.

3. Cook the wings for 35 minutes on the grill, rotating halfway through. After 35 minutes, check the interior temperature of the wings. It should be at least 165 degrees Fahrenheit.

Internal temp of 175- 180°F, on the other hand, will provide good quality.

4. Combine mustard, Franks Red-hot, & butter in a small skillet over medium heat for making the Red-hot Sauce of Franks. Cook, stirring regularly until the butter has melted & the sauce has reached room temperature. Set the wings aside & check them.

5. To make the Sauce of Sriracha Wing, mix Sriracha, sesame seed oil, soy sauce, and honey in a small skillet over medium heat. Cook, stirring until sauce is barely cooked through, whisk to mix. Place it aside.

6. Take the wings off the grill. Toss 1/3 of the chicken in a large mixing dish with the Red-hot sauce of Franks. Toss the remaining 1/3 of the salad with the Sriracha sauce. If preferred, season the remaining third of the wings with more Traeger Chicken Rub. Serve and have fun!

Roasted Buffalo Wings

Prep Time: 10 Minutes

Cook Time: 30 Minutes

Serves: 4 people

Ingredients

- Traeger Chicken Rub
- 1 Tablespoon of Cornstarch
- 4 Pound Chicken Wings Kosher Salt

Buffalo Sauce

- 1/2 Cup of Frank's Red-hot Sauce
- 6 Tablespoons of Unsalted Butter
- 1/4 Cup of Spicy Mustard

Instructions

1. Set the Traeger to 375°F & preheat for 15 minutes with the lid covered when ready to cook.

2. Dry the wings of the chicken with a paper towel while the grill is heating up. In a large mixing bowl, combine the wings, cornstarch, Traeger Chicken Rub, & salt to taste. Coat both halves of the chicken wings with the mixture.

3. Put the wings on the grill once it is hot & cook for 35 minutes, rotating halfway during the cooking time.

4. After 35 minutes, check the interior temperature of the wings. Internal temperature should be at least 165 degrees Fahrenheit. The internal temperature of 175-180°F, on the other hand, will provide good quality.

5. Combine the mustard, Franks, Red Hot, and butter in a saucepan to make the Buffalo Sauce. Combine all Ingredients

in a mixing bowl and cook on the burner until well heated. While the wings are cooking, keep the sauce warm.

6. Remove the wings from the grill and put them in a medium mixing bowl. Turn the wings with tongs to cover them with the buffalo sauce.

7. For the sauce to solidify, cook for another 10-15 mins on the grill. Wings should be served with a blue cheese dressing or ranch. Enjoy!

Smoked Turkey

Prep Time: 20 Minutes

Cook Time: 7 Hours

Serves: 6 people

Ingredients

- 1 Tablespoons of Canola Oil
- 1 1/2 Tablespoons of Minced Garlic
- 1 Cup of Sugar
- 1 (12-16 Lb.) Fresh or Frozen Turkey, Thawed, Giblets Removed
- 1 Cup of Traeger Rub
- 1/2 Cup of Worcestershire Sauce

Instructions

1. Fill a 5-gallon bucket (non-metal) with 3 gallons of water.
2. Mix in the Traeger rub, sugar, Garlic, and Worcestershire sauce until all sugars will be dissolved.
3. Place the turkey in the brine bucket with the breast side down. Ensure that the turkey is fully immersed in the water. Refrigerate the bucket overnight after covering it.
4. Take the turkey out of the brine and pat it dry. Place the turkey breast side in a disposable aluminium roasting pan and coat canola oil all over the outer sides.
5. Preheat the oven to 225 degrees Fahrenheit and cook for 15 minutes with the lid covered. If Super Smoke is available, use it for the best taste.
6. Put the turkey on the grill for about 2.5 to 3 hours to smoke.
7. Raise the grill temperature to 350°F and cook for 3.5 to 4

hours, or when the internal temperature of the breast reaches 165°F in the thickest section.

8. Remove the meat from the grill and set it aside for thirty minutes before carving. Enjoy!

Vietnamese Chicken Wings

Prep Time: 8 Hours

Cook Time: 1 Hour

Serves: 2 people

Ingredients

- 1 1/3 Tablespoons of Garlic, Minced
- 2 Tablespoons of Brown Sugar, Packed
- 1/8 Cup Ginger, Minced
- 2 Pound Chicken Wings
- 1/8 Cup Finely Chopped Shallot
- 2 Tablespoons of Scallion Whites, Chopped
- 1/3 Cup of Roughly Chopped Lemongrass Bottoms Fish Sauce
- 2 Tablespoons of Peanut Oil
- 2 Tablespoons of Lime Juice
- 1/8 Cup of Peanuts, Dry-Roasted, Chopped
- 1/8 Cup Cilantro, Finely Chopped
- 2/3 Teaspoon of Salt

Instructions

1. Remove the tips of the wings by splitting them at the junction. Using paper towels, gently dry the wings after rinsing them in cold water. Place in a large mixing basin and set aside.

2. In a food processor, puree the Garlic (roughly diced), shallots, scallions, ginger, lemongrass, brown sugar, lime juice, fish sauce, and peanut oil until smooth. Place the wings in a large resealable bag of plastic with the marinade. Refrigerate for at least one night.

3. Start the Traeger grill on smoke when you're ready to cook. Preheat for 5 minutes with the lid closed.

4. Take the wings out of the marinade and set them aside. Keep the marinade in a small saucepan & bring it to a boil before removing it from the heat. Brush the wings with this while they're cooking.

5. Put the wings on the grill & smoke for thirty min, seasoning with one teaspoon salt.

6. Raise the grill temperature to 350 degrees F after thirty min & roast for 40 - 50 minutes, flipping halfway through & brushing on the reserved sauce.

7. Remove the wings from the grill and put them on a serving dish with the peanuts & cilantro on top. Enjoy.

Spicy BBQ Whole Chicken

Prep Time: 15 Minutes

Cook Time: 3 Hours

Serves: 4 people

Ingredients

- 1 Onion
- 6 Thai Chiles
- 2 Tablespoons of Sugar
- 2 Tablespoons of Sweet Paprika
- 3 Tablespoons of Salt
- 4 Cups of Grapeseed Oil
- 1 Whole Chicken
- 5 cloves of Garlic
- 1 Scotch Bonnet Pepper

Instructions

1. Puree the Thai chilies, Scotch bonnet pepper, paprika, salt, sugar, onion, Garlic, & grapeseed oil in a blender or food processor until smooth.

2. Allow the chicken to rest in the fridge overnight after smothering it with the mixture.

3. When ready to cook, preheat the Traeger to 300°F with the lid closed for about 15 minutes.

4. Place the chicken breast side up on the grill & smoke for 3 hrs. Or until the interior temp of the breast reaches 165°F.

5. Remove the steak from the grill and set aside for 10 - 15 mins before slicing. Serve with your favorite sides. Enjoy!

Baked Garlic Parmesan Wings

Prep Time: 10 Minutes

Cook Time: 40 Minutes

Serves: 4 people

Ingredients

- 1 Cup of Butter
- 3 1/2 Tablespoons of Traeger Chicken Rub
- 5 Pound Chicken Wings
- 1/2 Cup of Unsalted Butter
- 10 cloves of Garlic, Minced
- 1 Cup of Shredded Parmesan Cheese
- 10 cloves of Garlic, Finely Diced
- 3 Tablespoons of Chopped Parsley

Instructions

1. Set the Traeger to 450°F & preheat for fifteen minutes with the lid covered when you're ready to cook.

2. Toss the wings of chicken with the Traeger Chicken Rub in a large mixing basin.

3. Cook for 20 minutes with the wings straight on the grate of the grill. Cook for another 20 minutes after flipping the wings.

4. Check the interior temperature of the wings; the finishing temperature should be between 165°F & 180°F.

5. To create the garlic sauce, mix the butter, Garlic, & leftover rub in a medium skillet and simmer over medium heat on top of the stove while the chicken is cooking. Cook by stirring continually for 8 - 10 mins.

6. Remove the wings from the grill and put them in a large mixing basin. Combine the wings, Parmesan cheese, garlic sauce, and parsley in a mixing bowl. Enjoy!

Roasted Rosemary Orange Chicken

Prep Time: 15 Minutes

Cook Time: 45 Minutes

Serves: 4 people

Ingredients

- 1 (3-4 Lb.) Chicken, Backbone Removed

Marinade

- 1/4 Cup Olive Oil
- 2 Teaspoons of Dijon Mustard
- 2 Oranges, Juiced
- 3 Tablespoons of Chopped Rosemary Leaves
- 2 Teaspoons of Kosher Salt
- 1 Orange, Zested

Instructions

1. Clean the chicken by rinsing it and patting it dry with paper towels.

2. To make the marinade, whisk together olive oil, orange juice (approximately 1/4 cup freshly squeezed), zest of orange, Dijon mustard, rosemary, & salt in a medium mixing bowl. To mix the Ingredients, whisk them together.

3. Put the chicken in a deep baking dish that will enable it to unfold in one piece completely. Pour the marinade over the chicken, making sure it is well coated.

4. Cover with plastic wrap & chill for at least 2 hours or up to 24 hours, rotating once throughout the procedure.

5. When ready to cook, preheat the Traeger to 350°F with the lid closed for fifteen minutes.

6. Retrieve the chicken from the marinade and put it skin-side down on the Traeger.

7. Cook for another 25 to 30 minutes, or until the skin is nicely browned. Continue to cook the chicken for another 5 to 15 minutes, or until the interior temperature of the breast hits 165°F & the thigh hits 175°F.

8. Allow 10 minutes to rest before slicing. Enjoy!

Traeger Crispy Orange Chicken Wings

Prep Time: 20 Minutes

Cook Time: 1 Hour

Serves: 2 people

Ingredients

- 1/4 Cup of Chicken Broth
- 2 Pound Chicken Wings Kosher Salt
- 1 Tablespoon of Asian Chili Garlic Sauce
- 1 Tablespoon of Cornstarch
- 1/3 Cup of Brown Sugar
- 1 Cup of Squeezed Orange Juice
- 1 Large Orange Zest
- 1 teaspoon of Ground Ginger
- 2 Tablespoons of Soy Sauce
- 1/4 Teaspoon of Black Pepper

Instructions

1. Set the Traeger to 350°F & preheat for fifteen min when you're ready to cook. Place chicken wings on a rack of wire drying over a sheet pan or maybe a sheet pan lined with towels of paper skin side up. To dry, blot with paper towels. Place wings in the fridge for at least an hour after seasoning with kosher salt.

2. To make the sauce, whisk together corn starch & chicken stock.

3. In a small saucepan, mix the remaining Ingredients & bring to a simmer on medium heat.

4. Stir in the corn starch & chicken stock slurry after the sauce has reached a boil. Continue to cook until the sauce thickens. Remove the pan from the heat & put it aside.

5. Cook for 45 minutes, or until the internal temperature reaches 170°F and the skin is golden brown.

6. Remove the wings from the grill and put them in a mixing dish with the orange sauce. Toss until all of the sauce has been absorbed by the wings. Have fun! Cooking times will vary based on the temperature you set and the ambient temperature.

Hellfire Grilled Chicken Wings

Prep Time: 15 Minutes

Cook Time: 40 Minutes

Serves: 4 people

Ingredients

- 1 Pound Chicken Wings
- 2 Tablespoons of Vegetable Oil
- 1 teaspoon of Onion Powder
- 1 teaspoon of Salt
- 1 Tablespoon of Paprika
- 2 Teaspoons of Brown Sugar
- 1 Teaspoon of Granulated Garlic
- 1 Teaspoon of Celery Seed
- 1 Teaspoon of Ground Black Pepper
- 1 teaspoon of Cayenne Pepper

Hot Sauce

- 4 Jalapeño Peppers, Sliced
- 8 Tablespoons of Unsalted Butter
- 1/2 Cup of Hot Sauce
- 1/2 Cup of Cilantro Leaves

Instructions

1. Remove the tips of the wings and throw them away. Each wing should be cut in half through the joint, resulting in a meaty drumette

2. & a flat. Pour oil over the chicken and move to a large mixing

bowl.

3. Combine the salt, paprika, sugar, black pepper, onion powder, cayenne, granulated Garlic, & celery seed in a small mixing bowl.

4. Toss the chicken wings lightly with your hands to coat them with the seasoning.

5. Preheat the Traeger to 350°F for 15 minutes with the lid closed when ready to cook.

6. Grill the wings for 35–40 minutes, or until skin is crisp & golden brown well as the chicken is well cooked. Halfway through the cooking time, turn once more.

7. To make the sauce, melt the butter in a small saucepan over medium- low heat. Cook for approximately 3 to 4 minutes after adding the jalapenos. Combine the cilantro & hot sauce in a mixing bowl.

8. Toss the wings in the sauce to coat them. Enjoy!

Jamaican Jerk Chicken

Active: 30 mins Total: 9 hrs. Yield: 8

Ingredients

- 1 onion, chopped
- 2 chills, chopped
- 3 scallions, chopped
- 2 garlic cloves, minced
- 1 teaspoon of thyme
- 1 tablespoon of spice powder
- 1 tablespoon of allspice berries
- 1 teaspoon of salt
- 1 tablespoon of ground pepper
- 1 tablespoon of vegetable oil
- 1 teaspoon of nutmeg
- Two -pound chickens, quartered
- 1/2 cup of soy sauce

Instructions

1. Combine the onion, chilies, scallions, Garlic, five-spice powder, pepper, allspice, thyme, nutmeg, & salt in a food processor; pulse until coarse paste forms. Add the soy sauce & oil in a constant stream while the machine is running. In a large dish, pour the marinade, add the chicken, and toss to coat.

2. Preheat the grill. Grill the chicken for 35 to 40 minutes over a moderate fire, turning periodically until nicely browned and cooked through. Lay the chicken on a serving dish and serve.

Pork recipes

Porchetta Classic (Smoked)

Prep Time: 30 Minutes

Cook Time: 2 Hours

Serves: 8 people

Ingredients

- 1 Teaspoon of Red Pepper Flakes

- 2 Tablespoons of Rosemary, Chopped

- 4 cloves of Garlic

- 2 Teaspoons of Salt

- 2 Pound (3 Lb.) Center-Cut Pork Loin

- 1 teaspoon of Black Pepper

- 6 Pound Skin-On Pork Belly Salt as per your taste

- Black Pepper as required

Instructions

1. Add minced garlic, rosemary, pepper, salt, & red pepper flakes in a medium mixing bowl to make the garlic combination.

2. Place the belly skin part upon the work surface (clean) & crosshatch the skin. Season the meat side of the belly with salt, pepper, & half of the mixture of garlic.

3. Place the trimmed pork in the belly's middle and massage the leftover garlic mixture, seasoning to taste.

4. Wrap the pork belly around the loin to create a cylindrical form & knot at 2 intervals. Flavour the skin with pepper and

salt, then place it in the refrigerator, uncovered, overnight to dry.

5. Set the temperature to 180°F & preheat for 10 minutes with the lid covered when ready to cook.

6. Put the Porchetta on the grill of the grate, seam side down, & smoke for an hour.

7. Raise that grill temperature to 325°F after an hour. Tent with foil if the outside starts to scorching before the required interior temp is achieved.

8. Remove the steak from the grill and set it aside for thirty minutes before cutting. Enjoy.

Smoked BBQ Ribs

Prep Time: 25 Minutes

Cook Time: 5 Hours

Serves: 4 people

Ingredients

- 1/4 Cup of Traeger Big Game Rub Traeger BBQ Sauce
- 1 Cup of Apple Juice
- 1 Rack St. Louis-Style Ribs

Instructions

1. Remove the membrane off the back of the ribs & pat them dry.

2. Rub the front, back, & sides of the ribs with an equal layer of rub. Allow for 20 minutes of setting time or up to 4 hours if refrigerated.

3. When ready to cook, preheat the Traeger to 225°F with the lid closed for fifteen min. If Super Smoke is available, use it for the best taste.

4. Place the ribs on the grill with the bone side down. After 1 hour of cooking, fill a spray bottle with apple juice & spray the ribs. After that, spray every 45 mins.

5. Check the interior temperature of the ribs after 4-1/2 hrs. When the internal temperature of the ribs hits 201°F, they are done. If not, wait another 30 mins and try again.

6. Brush a little coating of your preferred Traeger BBQ Sauce on the front & back of the ribs after they're done. Allow 10 minutes for the sauce to solidify.

7. Remove the ribs from the grill once the sauce has set and let them rest for ten minutes. Serve with additional sauce & ribs sliced in between the bones. Enjoy.

Garlic and Herb-Roasted Pork Tenderloin

Prep Time: 10 Minutes

Cook Time: 25 Minutes

Serves: 4 people

Ingredients

- Six cloves of Garlic, Peeled
- 1 Lemon Juice & Zest of Half, Remaining Half Thinly Sliced
- 1 Sprig Fresh Thyme, Stripped, Plus More for Garnish
- 1/4 Cup of Extra-Virgin Olive Oil, Plus More as Needed
- 2 (1 Lb. Each) Pork Tenderloins
- 1 Sprig Fresh Rosemary, Stripped, Plus More for Garnish
- 1 Pinch of Red Pepper Flakes (Optional)
- 1 Tablespoon of Soy Sauce
- 1 Teaspoon of Coarse Salt
- 1 1/2 Teaspoons of Freshly Ground Black Pepper

Instructions

1. Trim any excess fat or silver skin from both tenderloins using a sharp knife.

2. Mix the garlic, lemon zest, and juice, thyme, soy sauce, rosemary, salt, pepper, & red pepper flakes in the bowl of a blender or mini- food processor jar.

3. Pulse the garlic & herbs until they're finely minced. While the machine runs, slowly trickle in the olive oil until paste forms.

4. Apply the garlic paste to both tenderloins, being sure to coat all surfaces. Before grilling, wrap the pork firmly in plastic wrap & refrigerate for 8 hours.

5. Set the Traeger to 500°F & preheat for 15 minutes with the lid covered when you're ready to cook.

6. Preheat the grill to high and place the tenderloins straight on the grate. Roast for fifteen minutes.

7. Turn the tenderloins with tongs & continue to roast till the internal temperature reaches at least 145°F in the thickest section of the meat.

8. Allow the meat to rest for five minutes before slicing. Enjoy.

Pulled Pork Baked Potato Skins

Prep Time: 15 Minutes

Cook Time: 1 Hour

Serves: 6 people

Ingredients

- 4 Whole Potato

- Baker Style Vegetable Oil

- Salt as required

Canola Oil

- 4 Russet Potatoes

- 3 Cup Pulled Pork

- 2 Tablespoon Butter, Melted

- 4 Tablespoons of Traeger Sweet & Heat BBQ Sauce

- 1 Cup of Cheddar Cheese

- 1 Cup of Mozzarella Cheese Chopped Green Onion, For Serving

- Chopped Bacon, For Serving

- Sour Cream, For Serving

Instructions

1. Set the Traeger to 450°F and preheat for 15 minutes with the lid covered when you're ready to cook.

2. Coat potatoes with canola oil & season with salt equally. Place the potatoes straight on the grill grate & cook for 45 mins, or until a fork pricks them in the center and they are tender.

3. Hollow out the potatoes by cutting them in half and leaving 1/4" of potato on the skin. Place the skins on a baking pan and

brush the insides with melted butter. Return to the grill & cook for a further 5 to 6 minutes, until it's golden brown.

4. Combine the Traeger Sweet and Heat BBQ Sauce, pulled pork, mozzarella, & cheddar cheese in a large mixing bowl.

5. Fill the skins with mixture and return to the Traeger, lid closed, for just long enough for the cheese to melt.

6. Serve with chopped onions, bacon, & sour cream on the side. Enjoy.

Pulled Pork from a Smoked Traeger

Prep Time: 10 Minutes

Cook Time: 9 Hours

Serves: 8 people

Ingredients

- Traeger BBQ Sauce
- 1 Bone-In Pork Shoulder
- 1 cup of Apple Cider
- Traeger Pork and Poultry Rub

Instructions

1. When ready to cook, preheat the Traeger to 250°F with the lid closed for fifteen min.

2. Trim any extra fat from the pork butt while the Traeger heats up.

3. Season all sides with Traeger Pork and Poultry Rub and set aside for 20 minutes.

4. Place the fat of pork butt side up on the grill grate and cook for three to five hours, or until the interior temperature reaches 160°F.

5. Take the pork butt from the grill and set it aside.

6. Four big sheets of aluminum foil stacked on top of each other on a baking sheet, broad enough to cover the pork butt completely on both sides. If you don't have enough foil pieces, overlap them to make a larger foundation. Place the pig butt in the middle of the foil and pull up the sides a little before spilling the apple cider over top of it. Wrap the foil all around the pork firmly to prevent the cider from escaping.

7. Return the pork butt, foil-wrapped, to the grill, fat side up, &

cook until the interior temp of the thickest portion of the meat reaches 204°F, approximately 3 to 4 hours more, determined by the size of the big butt.

8. Remove the steaks from the grill. Let the pig rest in the foil package for 45 minutes.

9. Remove the pig from the foil & place it in a fat separator to drain any extra liquid.

10. Place the pig in a large mixing bowl and shred it, eliminating the bone and any extra fat. Return the separated liquid to the meat and season with more Traeger Big Game Rub to taste. Taste and season with Traeger 'Que BBQ Sauce and any preferred BBQ sauce, if desired.

11. Serve on its own, in your favorite dishes, or as a sandwich filling. Refrigerate leftover pork for up to 4 days in an airtight container. Enjoy.

BBQ Pulled Pork & Pork Belly

Prep Time: 4 Hours

Cook Time: 11 Hours

Serves: 4 people

Ingredients

- One cup Salt
- One Cup Brown Sugar
- 4 Pound Pork Belly, Skin Removed
- 10 Pound Bone-In Pork Butt
- 2 To Taste Salt
- 2 Tablespoons of Black Pepper
- 1 To Taste Black Pepper
- 1 1/2 cups of Apple Juice
- 1/2 Cup Onion, Small Diced
- 1 Tablespoon Sesame Oil
- 1 clove of Garlic, Minced
- 3/4 Cup of Tomato Sauce
- 2 Tablespoons of Ginger, Minced
- 2 Tablespoons of Soy Sauce
- 4 Tablespoon of Rice Vinegar
- 34 Tablespoons of Water
- 1/4 Cup of Thai Sweet Chili Sauce
- 1 Whole Daikon, Cut into Matchsticks
- 3 Whole Carrots, Cut into Matchsticks

- 2 Tablespoons of Sugar

- 2 Tablespoons of Sriracha

- 1 Whole Lime Juice

- 1 Cup of Mayonnaise

- 1 Whole Baguette, enough for 8 Sandwiches Sliced Lengthwise

- 1 Whole English Cucumber, Sliced Lengthwise

- 1 Bunch Cilantro, Leaves Picked

- 1 Whole Jalapeño, Sliced

Instructions

1. For the Belly of Pork, score the fat in a crosshatch pattern on the pork belly (about 1/4" deep). Rub pork belly with a mixture of salt, brown sugar, & black pepper. Refrigerate overnight after covering.

2. When ready to cook, preheat the grill on high for 15 minutes with the lid covered.

3. Cook for thirty minutes on the grill grate with the pork belly straight on it.

4. Reduce the heat to 275°F and cook for another 2 hours, or until a spear poked into the thickest portion glides in and out easily.

5. Trim any extra fat from the pig butt, leaving 1/4 inch of the fat cap intact for the pulled pork. In a small dish, combine 1 cup of apple juice, brown sugar, & 1 tablespoon salt, stirring until the salt and sugar are almost dissolved.

6. Inject the apple juice mixture into the butt of the pig every square inch. Season the pork butt with the remaining pepper and salt on the outside.

7. When ready to cook, preheat the Traeger to 250°F for 15

minutes with the lid closed.

8. Cook for approximately 6 hours, or until temp reaches 160°F, straight on the grill grate. Wrap the butt of pork in two pieces of aluminium foil & pour 1/2 cup apple juice over it. To keep the apple juice contained, wrap the tin foil firmly.

9. Raise the temperature to 275°F and return the pork butt to the grill in a pan big enough to catch any drips. Cook for 3 hours more, or until the internal temperature reaches 205°F.

10. Remove the bone from the grill & toss it out. Remove any extra fat or tendons from the pork and shred it. If required, season with more salt and pepper.

11. Heat sesame oil in a small saucepan over medium flame for the pulled pork sauce. Add the onion and cook for 1 to 2 minutes, or until transparent. Sauté garlic and ginger for 30 seconds, or until aromatic. Combine the tomato sauce, soy sauce, vinegar, water, and chilli sauce in a mixing bowl. Cook for 5 mins before turning off the heat. Pour over the shredded pork and toss to combine. Reserve.

12. To prepare the pickled veggies, put warm water, salt, sugar, and rice vinegar in a mixing bowl and whisk until the salt and sugar dissolve. Cover and chill for at least 4 hours after pouring the mixture over the matchstick veggies.

13. To make the Sriracha Mayo, whisk together all of the Ingredients until smooth. Around each side of cut bread, spread approximately two teaspoons of mayonnaise.

14. Line the sandwich with cucumber slices, onion slices, and jalapenos. Fill with sliced pork belly, daikon, pickled carrots, and cilantro, then top with a piece of the pulled pork. Serve right away. Enjoy.

Sandwich with BBQ Ribs

Prep Time: 15 Minutes

Cook Time: 3 Hours

Serves: 2 people

Ingredients

- 1 Cup of Traeger 'Que BBQ Sauce
- 3 Rack Baby Back Pork Ribs
- Cracked Black Pepper as per your taste
- Kosher Salt as per your taste
- 1 Jar Pickles
- 1 Yellow Onion, Sliced
- 4 Hoagie Rolls

Instructions

1. Remove the membrane from the rear of the ribs. Season with salt & cracked black pepper to taste.

2. When ready to cook, preheat the Traeger to 225°F for fifteen minutes with the lid closed.

3. Simmer for two hours with the meaty side up, then turn the ribs & cook for another hour with the meaty side down.

4. Remove the ribs from the grill and place them bone side up on a chopping board. Cut along the middle of each bone with a sharp knife & remove bones with your fingers.

5. Return the ribs to their original position & brush with half of Traeger's Que BBQ Sauce. Return to the grill for 5 to 10 mins to allow the sauce to solidify. Remove the steaks from the grill & put them aside.

6. Rib racks should be cut to fit the length of hoagie rolls. Place

the ribs on a bottom bun after splitting the hoagie buns in half.

7. Pickles, onions, additional BBQ sauce, as well as the top bun go on top. Enjoy.

Pork Loin Smoked

Prep Time: 5 Minutes

Cook Time: 3 Hours

Serves: 6 people

Ingredients

- Traeger Rub 1 Pork, Loins

Instructions

1. Traeger Rub is used to seasoning pork loin.

2. When ready to cook, preheat the grill to 180°F with the lid covered for 15 minutes.

3. Place the pork loin on a diagonal on the grill grates & smoke for 3 - 4 hrs.

4. Preheat the grill to 350°F & cook for 20 - 30 mins.

5. Remove the steaks from the grill and cut them into 1-1/2" steaks. Serve. Enjoy.

Smoked Pork Loin with Apples and Sauerkraut

Prep Time: 12 Minutes

Cook Time: 2 Hours

Serves: 4 people

Ingredients

- 1 Large Cooking Apples, Peeled and Sliced

- 1 Pork Loin Roast

Traeger Rub

- 1 Pound of Sauerkraut

- 1/2 Cup of Brown Sugar

- 1 Whole Bay Leaves

- 1 Cup of Dark Beer

- 1 Onion, Sliced

- 1 Tablespoon of Butter

Instructions

1. Set that Traeger to 150°F and preheat for almost fifteen min with the lid covered when you're ready to cook. If Super Smoke is available, use it for the best taste.

2. Season that pork loin with the Traeger Rub or black pepper & salt on both surfaces. Put the roast on the grill grates straight, cover, & smoke for an hour.

3. Layer the sauerkraut, onions, apples, beer, brown sugar, butter, & bay leaves in the large oven or baking dish. Right on top of a sauerkraut mix, place the smoked pork loin. Using a cover or a sheet of foil, cover the pan.

4. Bring the pan to the grill & raise the temperature to 360°F on

the Traeger. Close the top and roast that pork for another hour, or till a thermometer register 160°F.

5. Allow time for the roast to rest on a chopping board. Meanwhile, toss the sauerkraut mix gently & serve on the serving dish. Layer the sauerkraut & apples on top of the roast pork slices. Enjoy.

Paleo Pork Spare Ribs on the BBQ

Prep Time: 15 Minutes

Cook Time: 4 Hours

Serves: 4 people

Ingredients

Rub

- 1 Tablespoons of Coarse Ground Black Pepper
- 4 Tablespoons of Paprika
- 2 Tablespoons of Onion Powder
- 1 Teaspoon of Chipotle Chile Powder
- 1 Tablespoon of Garlic Powder
- 4 Tablespoons of Kosher Salt
- 2 Rack St. Louis-Style Ribs
- 1/2 Cup of Water

BBQ Sauce

- 15 Fluid Ounce Organic Tomato Sauce
- 1/2 Cup of Apple Cider Vinegar
- 1/3 Cup of Sweet Honey
- 1 teaspoon of Paprika
- 2 Teaspoons of Onion Powder
- 1 1/2 Teaspoons of Coarse Ground Black Pepper
- 1 Teaspoon of Ground Mustard

Instructions

1. When ready to cook, preheat the Traeger to 225°F for 15

minutes with the lid closed. If Super Smoke is available, use it for the best taste.

2. Combine all rub components in a small dish.

3. Remove the membrane from the back of the ribs & massage the rub on both sides. Allow 15 to 20 mins for the ribs to rest.

4. Place the ribs bone-side down on the grill & cook for about 4 to 4-1/2 hrs. Check the ribs' interior temperature; the ideal temperature is 202°F. Cook for a further thirty min or until the temp reaches the desired level.

5. Prepare the sauce while the ribs are cooking. To make the sauce, combine all Ingredients in a saucepan and cook through on the stovetop.

6. Apply a thin coat of sauce to both sides of the ribs & simmer for another 10 minutes to allow the sauce to solidify.

7. Before slicing, remove the ribs from the grill and then let them rest for 10 minutes. Enjoy.

Traeger Pulled Pork Sandwiches

Prep Time: 15 Minutes

Cook Time: 11 Hours

Serves: 8 people

Ingredients

- Traeger Pork and Poultry Rub

- 2 cups of Apple Juice

- 1 (5-7 Lb.) Bone-In Pork Shoulder Traeger BBQ Sauce

- Coleslaw, For Serving

- 10 Hamburger Buns

Instructions

1. Season both sides of the pork roast with Traeger Pork and Poultry rub.

2. When ready to cook, preheat the Traeger to 225°F with the lid closed for fifteen min. If Super Smoke is available, use it for the best taste.

3. Place the roast fat-side up on the grill grate & smoke for 3 hours. After the first hour, spray roast with the apple juice per hour.

4. Transfer the pork to a throwaway aluminium foil pan big enough to accommodate the roast after three hours. Increase the grill temp to 250°F and cook for another 6 to 8 hours, or till a thermometer placed in the thickest part of the flesh, but not contacting bone, reads 203°F. Cover the pork loosely with aluminium foil if it begins to brown too much.

5. Place the pork roast on a chopping board and set aside for 20 minutes to rest. Fill a gravy separator halfway with the juices from the base of the pan. Any fat that has risen to the top

should be discarded.

6. Pull the pork into pieces with both hands (ideally wearing heavy-duty, lined rubber gloves to protect the hands from the heat). Discard the bone, as well as any fat lumps, along with the cap. Transfer each piece to a large mixing basin and shred it.

7. Season with more rub & moisten with the pork liquid you set aside. Mix your preferred Traeger BBQ sauce with the pulled pork.

8. Serve with coleslaw and the pork mixture on hamburger buns. Enjoy.

Spare Ribs of Smoked Pork

Prep Time: 15 Minutes

Cook Time: 4 Hours

Serves: 8 people

Ingredients

- 1 Rack Pork Ribs, Trimmed
- 1 Cup of Apple Juice
- 9 Ounce of Traeger BBQ Sauce
- 3 Tablespoons of Traeger Pork & Poultry Rub

Instructions

1. When preparing to cook, preheat the Traeger to 250°F.

2. Peel the silver skin off the ribs & trim any extra fat if the butcher hasn't already done so.

3. Traeger Pork and Poultry Rub should be used on both sides of the ribs.

4. Place the extra ribs bone part racks down on the grill grates & cook for 3 to 5 hrs. Drizzle the ribs with some apple juice after an hour. After just that, continue spraying with some apple juice each hour.

5. After two hours, start monitoring the temperature. After 3 to 5 hours, the interior temperature must be 203°F.

6. Coat the ribs on both sides in BBQ sauce of the choice when the internal temperature reaches 210°F. Return the ribs to grill & cook for another 30 to 50 minutes to let the sauce thicken.

7. Cut all slabs into two or into separate ribs to serve with the extra BBQ sauce. Enjoy.

Pork with Grilled Lemon

Prep Time: 20 Minutes

Cook Time: 20 Minutes

Serves: 4 people

Ingredients

- 1 Clove of Garlic, Minced

- 1/2 Teaspoon of Kosher Salt

- 1 Teaspoon of Freshly Parsley

- 2 Lemons, Zested

- 2 Tablespoons of Olive Oil

- 1 Teaspoon of Lemon Juice

- 1/4 Teaspoon of Black Pepper

- 1 (2 Lb.) Pork Tenderloin

Instructions

1. Everything but the tenderloin should be whisked together in a small basin.

2. Trim the tenderloin of any silver skin or extra fat.

3. Pork should be placed in a big resealable bag. Zip the tenderloin shut after pouring the marinade over it. Refrigerate for at least two hours but not more than eight hours.

4. Set the Traeger to 375°F & preheat for fifteen min with the lid covered when you're ready to cook.

5. Take the tenderloin out of the bag and throw away the marinade.

6. When the grill is heated, put the tenderloin straight on the grate & cook for 15 to 20 minutes, turning halfway through,

until the internal temperature reaches 145 degrees F.

7. Remove the pan from the heat & set it aside to cool for 5 to 10 mins before slicing. Enjoy.

Pork Belly on the BBQ

Prep Time: 15 Minutes

Cook Time: 3 Hours

Serves: 6 people

Ingredients

- 2 Tablespoons of Salt
- Traeger Pork and Poultry Rub
- 1/2 Teaspoon Black Pepper
- 1 (3 Lb.) Pork Belly, Skin Removed

Instructions

1. Set the Traeger to 275°F and warm for 15 minutes with the lid closed when ready to cook.

2. Season both sides of the pork belly with salt, pepper, & Traeger Pork and Poultry Rub in the meanwhile. Cook for 3 - 3-1/2 hrs. Or until the interior temperature reaches 200°F, straight on the grill grate.

3. Before slicing, remove the steak from the grill and set it aside for 10 to 15 minutes.

4. Serve in tacos, mac & cheese, nachos, or any other meal that you want. Enjoy.

Spare Ribs of Sweet Peach

Ingredients

- 4 Rack Pork Spare Ribs Apple Juice, For Spritzing Traeger Pork & Poultry Rub

- 1 Tablespoon of Butter

- 1 1/2 Cup of Peach Preserves 1 Onion, Chopped

- 1 Cup of Light Corn Syrup

- 1/2 Cup of Apple Cider Vinegar

- 1/2 Cup of Bourbon

- 1 Teaspoon of Grated Ginger

- 1 teaspoon of Worcestershire Sauce

- 1 Clove of Garlic, Minced

- 1 Teaspoon of Dry Mustard

Instructions

1. Remove any extra fat by wiping the ribs with wet paper towels. Traeger Pork and Poultry Rub are applied on both sides of the ribs.

2. Set the Traeger to 275°F & preheat for fifteen min with the lid closed when ready to cook. Use Super Smoke if it's available for the best taste.

3. Cook the ribs for 3 hours, bone-side down, on a rib rack, or straight on the barbecue grate, sprinkling with apple juice for 30 to 45 minutes.

4. In a medium saucepan set over a moderate flame, melt the butter. Cook until the onion is golden brown. Add the peach preserves, vinegar, corn syrup, bourbon, & Worcestershire sauce and whisk to combine. Mix thoroughly after adding the

ginger, mustard, and garlic. Cook for 15 minutes, till the sauce thickens.

5. Reduce the Traeger's temperature to 165 degrees Fahrenheit after 3 hours. Mist the ribs with apple juice per 30 minutes while smoking for 1 1/2 to 2 hours.

6. To complete, raise the temperature of the Traeger to 275°F for ten minutes. Remove the ribs from the grill and brush on peach sauce generously. Enjoy.

Pork Belly with Brown Sugar BBQ

Prep Time: 15 Minutes

Cook Time: 3 Hours

Serves: 8 people

Ingredients

- 1 (3-4 Lb.) Pork Belly
- 4 Tablespoons of Salt
- 4 Tablespoons of Brown Sugar

Instructions

1. Take the pork belly out of the fridge & blot it dry using paper towels the night before you intend to cook. Score fat in a diamond pattern with a sharp knife. Be careful not to cut the flesh.

2. Rub pork belly on both sides with a salt-and-brown-sugar mixture. Refrigerate uncovered overnight after placing on a drying rack on a pan.

3. Remove pork belly from refrigerator 30 mins before cooking. Rinse with cold water and blot with paper towels until completely dry.

4. Set the Traeger to 450°F & preheat for 15 minutes with the lid closed when ready to cook.

5. For 30 minutes, place the pork belly fat side up directly on the grill grate.

6. Reduce the heat to 325°F after 30 minutes & cook for another 3 hours, or until the pork is soft and the fat is crisp.

7. Allow 30 minutes to rest before slicing after removing from the grill.

8. Serve with baked beans, coleslaw, potato salad, white bread, BBQ sauce, and other BBQ favourites. Enjoy.

Paleo Vinegar Sauce for BBQ Pulled Pork

Ingredients

- 4 Tablespoons of Honey Paleo Vinegar BBQ Sauce
- 1 Tablespoon of Frank's Red-hot Sauce
- 1/2 Teaspoon of Coarse Ground Black Pepper
- 1 Teaspoon of Red Pepper Flakes
- 2 cup Apple Cider Vinegar

Main

- 1 teaspoon of Kosher Salt
- 6 Tablespoons of Paprika
- 1 (6-10 Lb.) Pork Butt
- 2 Teaspoons of Kosher Salt
- 1 Teaspoon Mustard Powder
- 1 teaspoon of Garlic Powder
- 2 Teaspoons of Pepper
- 1 Teaspoon of Ground Sage
- 1 Teaspoon of Cinnamon
- 1/2 Cup of Unsweetened Apple Juice
- 1/2 Teaspoon of Coarse Ground Black Pepper

Instructions

1. Set the Traeger to 225°F and warm for 15 minutes with the lid closed when ready to cook.

2. To make the sauce, combine all the Ingredients. Sauce may be prepared up to two days ahead of time and stored in the refrigerator until needed.

3. Mix all of the rub's components. Pork should be defatted. Using a coating of the rub on the pork, season it. Allow for a 20-minute recovery period.

4. Cook for 4-1/2 hours with the pork butt straight on the grill grate. Check the pork's internal temperature after 4-1/2 hours; it should be between 155- and 165-degrees F. If it isn't, wait 30 minutes and check again.

5. Wrap the pork inside the second layer of aluminium foil heavy- duty when the temperature hits 155-165°F. Back on the grill, pour the apple juice into the foil package containing the meat.

6. Cook for another 3 hours at 250°F before checking the internal temperature. In the thickest portion of the pork, a temperature of 204-206°F is ideal. Check the pork every half an hour till it reaches 204-206°F.

7. Depending on the amount of pork, the whole cook time must be between 8 and 10 hours.

8. Remove the bone as well as any extra fat by pulling or shredding the pork. Pour the sauce over the meat for taste. Enjoy.

Vegetables and Sides

Roasted Asparagus

Prep Time: 5 Minutes

Cook Time: 20 Minutes

Serving: 4

Ingredients

- 1 Bunch of Asparagus
- Traeger rub for Veggie
- 2 Tablespoon of Olive Oil

Instructions

1. Toss asparagus with the olive oil and the Traeger Veggie Rub, making sure all pieces are well coated.

2. Set the Traeger to almost 350°F and heat for fifteen minutes with the lid covered when ready to cook.

3. For 20 to 30 minutes, put asparagus straight on the grill grate.

Grilled Romaine Salad with Blue-Bacon Dressing

Prep Time: 5 Minutes

Cook Time: 20 Minutes

Serving: 2

Ingredients

- 1 Lettuce Heart Pinch of Salt
- 1 Teaspoon of Olive Oil
- Fresh Black Pepper
- A tablespoon of Garlic Powder
- 2 Teaspoon of grated Parmesan Cheese Blue-Cheese Dressing
- 2 Teaspoon of Mayonnaise
- 2 Teaspoon of Blue Cheese
- 1/4 Cup of Milk

Instructions

1. Set the Traeger to the 450°F
2. After cutting the romaine in half, brush or sprinkle olive oil across both sides. Salt, pepper to taste, and Parmesan cheese are used to season the lettuce.
3. Place the romaine lettuce pressing down on the grill grate.
4. Withdraw the grill from the heat after 2 minutes. In a large mixing bowl, combine blue cheese, mayo, and milk.
5. Season with salt, pepper to taste, and garlic powder to taste good.
6. Toss in some bacon. Assemble the salad and top with additional blue cheese if preferred. Relish!

Grilled Corn with Honey Butter & Smoked Salt

Prep Time: 15 Minutes

Cook Time: 10 Minutes

Serving: 4

Ingredients

- 6 Pieces of Corn, Husked
- 1/2 Cup of Butter, Room Temperature
- 2 Tablespoon of Olive Oil
- 1/2 Cup of Honey
- 1 teaspoon of Black Pepper
- 1 Tablespoon of Smoked Salt

Instructions

1. Set the temperature to Medium and warm for 15 minutes with the lid covered when prepared to cook.

2. Brush the corn with the oil and sear it, flipping it once in a while. Corn must be done through and lightly browned from the outside after around 10 minutes.

3. Whisk butter and the honey together for about 1 minute in the mixing bowl until smooth and creamy.

4. Brush heated corn over the top after removing it from the bowl. Garnish with ground pepper and Jacobson smoky salt. Cooking times will vary based on the temperature of the set and the surrounding temperature.

Roasted Cauliflower with Parmesan Garlic Butter

Prep Time: 12 Minutes

Cook Time: 35 Minutes

Serving: 4

Ingredients

- 1/4 Cup of Olive Oil

- 1 Head Cauliflower

- Some salt and grounded pepper

- 1/4 Cup of Shredded Parmesan Cheese

- 1/2 Cup of Melted Butter

- 1 Cloves of Minced Garlic

- 1/2 Tablespoon of Chopped Parsley

Instructions

1. When set to cook, heat the Traeger to the 450 degrees Fahrenheit with the lid covered for fifteen min.

2. Sprinkle the cauliflower with some salt and black pepper after brushing it with olive oil.

3. Inside a cast iron pan, lay the cauliflower immediately upon that grill grate and heat for 30 min, or till golden brown and soft in the center.

4. In a medium bowl, mix the softened butter, cheese, garlic, and chopped parsley, whereas the cauliflower is heating.

5. Braise the cauliflower with that melting butter mixture in the last 30 minutes of simmering.

6. Retrieve the cauliflower from either the grill and, if wanted, sprinkle with more cheese and parsley. Dig!

Grilled Peach and Bacon Salad with Maple Vinaigrette

Prep Time: 10 Minutes

Cook Time: 20 Minutes

Serving: 4

Ingredients

- 1 Tablespoon of Maple Syrup
- 2 medium Peaches, Firm but ripe
- 2 Cup of Arugula
- 1/4 Cup of Toasted Pecans
- 1/4 Cup of Feta Cheese
- 1/4 Cup of Bacon, Chopped, and Cooked

Dressing

- 1 medium Shallot, Chopped 3 Tablespoon of Olive Oil
- 2 Tablespoon of Maple Syrup 1 Teaspoon of Curry Powder
- 1 Tablespoon of Apple Cider Vinegar
- 1/2 Teaspoon of Salt

Instructions

1. When set to cook, heat the Traeger to the 425°F with the lid shut for fifteen minutes.

2. Eventually, remove the pit from the peaches and cut them in half.

3. Put cut-side downward on the grill grates and drizzle with the maple syrup. Cook for 15–20 minutes, or till grill marks develop on the surface. Remove the steaks from the grill and set them aside to chill.

4. Mix all the dressing Ingredients in a small dish and put them

aside.

5. Inside a large mixing basin, combine all the salad Ingredients. Grilled peaches should be sliced and placed on top.

6. Pour the salad with that curry maple dressing and then season to taste. Share and have great times!

Smoked Macaroni Salad

Prep Time: 15 Minutes

Cook Time: 20 Minutes

Serving: 4

Ingredients

- 1/2 Red Onion, finely diced
- 1 Pound of Elbow Macaroni
- 1 big Bell Pepper, chopped
- 1 Cup of Mayonnaise
- 1/2 Cup of Shredded Carrots
- 3 Tablespoon of White Wine Vinegar
- Pinch of Salt
- 2 Tablespoon of Sugar
- Some Black Pepper

Instructions

1. Prepare pasta as per package Instructions in a big stock saucepan containing salted water over medium-high heat. Cook until the pasta is al dente, then drain and wash under cool water.

2. Set the Traeger to 190°F and heat for fifteen minutes with the lid covered when ready to cook. If Extra Smoke is available, use it for the best flavour.

3. Put a sheet tray upon the grill grate and pour out the cooked spaghetti on it. Cook for 25 minutes, then take from the flame and place in the refrigerator to chill.

4. Stir the dressing when the pasta has been cooling down.

Whisk together the mayo, the wine vinegar, and sugar in such a medium mixing bowl. To taste, sprinkle with salt and pepper.

5. In a large mixing bowl, add chopped vegetables, smoky pasta, and dressing once the pasta has cooled.

6. Refrigerate for 30 minutes before serving, covered in plastic wrap. Adore!

Roasted Green Beans with Bacon

Prep Time: 5 Minutes

Cook Time: 20 Minutes

Serving: 4

Ingredients

- 1 1/2 Pound of Green Beans, Edges Trimmed
- 4 Tablespoon of Extra-Virgin Olive Oil
- 4 Strips of Bacon, sliced Into Small Pieces
- 2 Clove of Garlic, Minced
- 1 teaspoon of Kosher Salt

Instructions

1. When prepared to cook, preheat the Traeger to 350°F with the lid shut for fifteen minutes.
2. Mix all of the Ingredients and distribute them out uniformly on the sheet tray.
3. Set the tray straight upon this grill grate and cook for twenty minutes, or until bacon becomes crispy as well as the beans are gently browned. Dig!

Roasted Broccoli with Parmesan

Prep Time: 5 Minutes

Cook Time: 10 Minutes

Serving: 6

Ingredients

- 2 Tablespoon of Lemon Juice
- 6 Cup of Fresh Broccoli, diced Into Bite-Sized Chunks
- 2 Tablespoon of Olive Oil
- 1/4 Teaspoon of Salt
- 1 Clove of Garlic, Minced
- 1/4 Teaspoon of Pepper
- 1/4 Cup of Parmesan Cheese

Instructions

1. Fill a big zippered bag halfway with broccoli.
2. Sprinkle the broccoli with lemon juice, cooking oil, garlic, kosher salt, and pepper, gently toss to cover. Allow for 30 minutes of resting time.
3. Set the Traeger to 375°F and heat for fifteen minutes with the lid covered when set to cook.
4. To keep the broccoli from sticking to the grill or falling from the grates, place it in a grilling pan or even on the sheet pan. Cook 10 to 15 minutes on the grill, or till crisp but soft. Remove from the oven and top with Parmesan cheese. Enjoy!

Roasted Sweet Potato Fries

Prep Time: 15 Minutes

Cook Time: 30 Minutes

Serving: 4

Ingredients

- 3 Tablespoon of Extra-Virgin Olive Oil
- 4 medium Sweet Potatoes, Peeled, rinsed, and sliced Into Fries
- 1 Tablespoon of Salt
- 1 Cup of Mayonnaise
- 1 teaspoon of Black Pepper
- 2 pieces of Chipotle Peppers in the Adobo Sauce
- 2 medium Limes, Juiced

Instructions

1. Set the Traeger to 500°F and heat for fifteen minutes with the lid covered when set to cook.

2. Distribute the sweet potatoes evenly over a baking sheet and brush with olive oil, kosher salt, and pepper.

3. Put this sheet pan over the grill grates and grill for 15 to 20 minutes, till the potatoes are golden and crispy, flipping periodically.

4. Mash the mayonnaise, chillies, and lime juice inside a blender until creamy, whereas the potatoes keep on cooking.

5. Serve these fries with a sprinkle of chipotle mayonnaise on the top or even on the sideline for dipping. Dig!

Grilled Asparagus & Honey Carrots

Prep Time: 15 Minutes

Cook Time: 35 Minutes

Serving: 4

Ingredients

- 1 Pound of Carrot, Peeled Some Lemon Zest
- 1 Bunch of Asparagus
- 2 Tablespoon of Olive Oil
- 2 Tablespoon of Honey Some Sea Salt

Instructions

1. All veggies should be rinsed in ice water. Pour olive oil over asparagus and season generously with kosher salt. Pour honey over the carrots and season with a pinch of salt.

2. Heat the Traeger to 350°F for fifteen minutes with the lid shut when prepared to cook.

3. Sauté the carrots initially for 15-25 minutes on a grill. Next, add the asparagus and simmer for yet another 20 to 30 minutes, or until they're ready.

4. Serve the asparagus with a sprinkling of grated lemon zest. Dig!

Mashed Red Potatoes

Prep Time: 15 Minutes

Cook Time: 40 Minutes

Serving: 4

Ingredients

- 8 medium Red Potatoes Grounded Black Pepper
- Pinch of Salt
- 1/4 Cup of Butter
- 1/2 Cup of Heavy Cream

Instructions

1. Set the temperature to 180°F and heat for fifteen minutes with the lid covered when prepared to cook.

2. Red potatoes should be sliced in half lengthwise and then in half yet again to create quarters. Season the potatoes using salt and black pepper.

3. Raise the fire to maximum and heat the oven. Put potatoes straight on the grill grates when the grill is heated.

4. To ensure that both sides of the potatoes acquire color, turn them every 15 minutes. Carry on in this manner until the potatoes become fork crisp

5. Mash potatoes with some cream, butter, kosher salt, and pepper to flavour until they're soft. Warm it up and enjoy it!

Baked Garlic Duchess Potatoes

Prep Time: 30 Minutes

Cook Time: 1 Hour

Serving: 8

Ingredients

- 12 large Potatoes
- 5 medium Egg Yolk
- Grounded Black Pepper
- Pinch of Salt
- 2 cloves of Garlic, Minced
- 3/4 Cup of Sour Cream
- 1 Cup of Heavy Cream
- 10 Tablespoon of Butter, Melted

Instructions

1. Fill a big saucepan halfway with water and add the potatoes. Sprinkle with salt and pepper. Over moderate flame, bring to the boil.

2. Lower heat to low and cook for 30 to 50 minutes, or until the paring knife readily slips into potatoes. Drain and set aside to cool.

3. Heat the Traeger to 450°F for fifteen minutes with the lid shut when prepared to cook.

4. Gently mix egg yolks, garlic, butter, sour cream, and black pepper in the large mixing bowl. Season with salt and pepper.

5. Potatoes should be peeled, and the flesh pushed through the ricer or grain mill straight into the bowl containing the beaten eggs. Carefully mix in the beaten eggs, taking good care not to overmix them.

6. Bake for 30–40 minutes, preferably golden brown and somewhat puffy, in the 3-quart cooking dish. Enjoy!

Smoked Yummy Olives

Prep Time: 10 Minutes

Cook Time: 20 Minutes

Serving: 4

Ingredients

- 1 Quart of Extra-Virgin Olive Oil
- 1 Pound of Mixed Olives
- 1 Whole of Orange Zest
- 1/2 Tablespoon of Red Pepper
- 1 medium Lemon Zest
- 1/2 Tablespoon of Dried Fennel Seed
- 4 large Thyme Sprigs
- 3 medium Dried Bay Leaves
- 4 large Rosemary Sprigs

Instructions

1. When set to cook, turn that Traeger grill on the Smoke and keep the flame at that settings.

2. Put the olives on a baking pan and cook them. Grill the olives for 15 to 20 minutes, or till they have a Smokey taste.

3. When these olives have reached the appropriate level of smokiness, remove them off the grill and set them aside to cool. After the smoked olives have cooled, mix them with the olive oil, oranges and lemon zest, chilli flakes, fennel, some bay leaves, some thyme, and rosemary. Preserve inside an airtight jar with all of the olives immersed.

4. Serve with one's favourite side dishes or even as a major part

of a Traeger Spread. Cheers!

Roasted Root Vegetables

Prep Time: 15 Minutes

Cook Time: 45 Minutes

Serving: 6

Ingredients

- 1 Bunch of Red Beets, washed And Trimmed
- 1 Butternut Squash, trimmed And Seeded
- 1 Bunch of Golden Beets, washed And Trimmed
- 1 medium Yam, Peeled
- 1 medium Red Onion, Peeled
- 1 medium Carrot, Peeled
- 4 cloves of Garlic, Peeled
- 1 large Cinnamon Stick
- 3 Tablespoons of Fresh Thyme Leaves
- 3 Tablespoons of Extra-Virgin Olive Oil
- Grounded Black Pepper
- Pinch of Salt
- 2 Tablespoon of Honey

Instructions

1. When set to cook, heat the Traeger approximately to 450°F for fifteen minutes with the lid shut.

2. Vegetables should be sliced into 1/2-inch pieces. Toss veggies with garlic cloves, thyme leaves, extra virgin olive oil, and cinnamon stick in the large mixing bowl.

3. Line another baking pan with aluminium foil. Spread the

veggies in one layer on a baking tray and season well with salt and black pepper.

4. Vegetables should be roasted on either the Traeger for 30 mins or until soft. When the vegetables are tender, put in the serving dish and sprinkle them with honey. Serve warm. Enjoy!

Roasted Sheet Pan Vegetables

Prep Time: 10 Minutes

Cook Time: 25 Minutes

Serving: 4

Ingredients

- 1 Small Head of Yellow Cauliflower, sliced into 3 Inch Florets
- 1 Small Head of Purple Cauliflower, sliced into 3 Inch Florets
- 4 Cup of Butternut Squash
- 3 Tablespoon of Olive Oil
- 2 Cup of Oyster Mushrooms, washed And Sliced
- 2 teaspoons of Kosher Salt
- 1/4 Cup of Chopped Flat-Leaf Parsley
- Freshly Grounded Black Pepper

Instructions

1. Set the Traeger to 450°F and heat for fifteen minutes with the lid covered when ideal for cooking.

2. Mix all of the veggies in a big mixing bowl. Sprinkle olive oil on top, then season with sea salt and freshly ground black pepper.

3. Toss the veggies with your hands till they are uniformly covered.

4. Spread the vegetables out again on 1 or 2 half tray sheets or cooking sheets, leaving some space between them. (Whether they are overcrowded, the veggies will steam rather than roast, and the crunchy texture will be lost.)

5. Cook for fifteen minutes upon that Traeger with the sheet pans. Fully open and toss, then cover the top and simmer for another 15 to 30 minutes, or until the veggies are golden

around the sides.

6. Serve shortly after tossing with parsley. At ambient
   temperature, the veggies are equally cooked. Enjoy!

Grilled Buffalo Blue Cheese Corn

Prep Time: 15 Minutes

Cook Time: 15 Minutes

Serving: 8

Ingredients

- 1/2 Cup of Hot Sauce

- 1 Cup of Crumbled Blue Cheese

- 8 Pieces of Ears Corn

- 1/2 Cup of Butter

- Some Celery Salt

Instructions

1. Set the heat to Maximum and warm for fifteen minutes with the lid covered when prepared to cook.

2. As the grill is heating up, combine the butter and that hot sauce inside a medium oven-proof pan and set on the grill grates to soften the butter. To mix the Ingredients, whisk them together. Remove from the oven and keep it warm.

3. Set the corn over the grill grates and cook for 5 minutes on each side, rotating with tongs as required till the corn is gently browned in parts.

4. Place the corn on a plate, a disposable plastic foil pan, or even a covered baking sheet.

5. Coat the corn on both sides with either butter or spicy sauce mix, placing in the pan.

6. Season with a pinch of celery salt, and top with diced blue cheese. Serve right away. Enjoy!

Grilled Corn on the Cob with Parmesan and Garlic

Prep Time: 5 Minutes

Cook Time: 30 Minutes

Serving: 6

Ingredients

- 1 cloves of Garlic, Minced
- 4 Tablespoons of Butter, Melted
- Pinch of Salt and Pepper
- 1/2 Cup of Shaved Parmesan
- 8 Ears of Fresh Corn
- 1 Tablespoon of Chopped Parsley

Instructions

1. Set the Traeger to 460°F and heat for fifteen minutes with the lid covered when ideal for cooking.

2. In a large mixing bowl, combine the butter, garlic, table salt, and pepper.

3. Pull the silk from the corn husks by peeling them back. Half of that garlic butter concoction should be rubbed on the corn.

4. Put the husks over the grill grates and close. Cook, stirring periodically, for 30 to 35 minutes, or till corn is soft.

5. Take the husks from the grill and discard them. Put corn on a serving platter and sprinkle with the leftover butter, parmesan, and fresh parsley and have great fun!

Artichokes with Gribiche Sauce

Prep Time: 25 Minutes

Cook Time: 25 Minutes

Serving: 4

Ingredients

- 1 Cup of Mayonnaise
- 3 medium Globe Artichokes, Cut & Cooled
- 1 Cup of Whole Milk Yogurt
- 2 Tablespoon of Chopped Flat-Leaf Parsley
- 2 Tablespoon of Dill Pickle, properly Chopped
- 2 Tablespoons of Capers, Drained
- 1 Teaspoon of Chopped Thyme
- 1 Tablespoon of Finely Chopped Shallot
- 2 Medium Boiled Eggs, finely Chopped
- 1 Cup of Panko Breadcrumbs, Toasted
- Pinch of Salt and Pepper
- Medium Lemon, Juiced
- 3 Tablespoons of Extra-Virgin Olive Oil

Instructions

1. Boil artichokes in gently seasoned water for 40 minutes in a big saucepan. Allow cooling before slicing in half.

2. Heat the oven to 375 degrees F and leave the lid covered for 15 minutes when prepared to cook.

3. Mix the mayo, yoghurt, pickles, chopped parsley, shallots, capers, thyme, lemon juice, salt and pepper, eggs to flavour in

a large bowl to create the gribiche sauce. Mix until everything is well combined.

4. Brush the artichokes using olive oil, sprinkle with salt and black pepper, and grill for fifteen minutes or rich golden brown.

5. Extract the choke, transfer to a tray, top with some bread crumbs, and garnish with that gribiche sauce. Dig!

Christmas Sprouts

Prep Time: 15 Minutes

Cook Time: 50 Minutes

Serving: 6

Ingredients

- 1 large Onion, Diced

- 1/2 Pound of Thick-Cut Bacon

- 2 Pound of Fresh Brussels sprouts

- Pinch of Salt and Pepper

- 2 Tablespoons of Olive Oil

Instructions

1. Preheat the oven to 250 degrees F and leave the lid covered for five to ten minutes when prepared to cook.

2. Sauté for 15-20 minutes, or till bacon is gently browned, straight on the grill grate. Just take off the grill and place it on a dish lined with paper towels.

3. In a big measuring bowl, cut onion in halves and afterwards slice into 15-inch moons. Put brussels sprouts into the bowl after slicing them in half longitudinally.

4. Add the 12-inch chunks of saved bacon to the bowl. Sprinkle olive oil over the top and sprinkle with salt. Dump into the cooking pan after tossing to coat.

5. Preheat the grill to 350 degrees Fahrenheit and set the cooking pan on it. Simmer for 30 minutes with constant stirring.

Smoked Jalapeño Poppers

Prep Time: 15 Minutes

Cook Time: 1 Hour

Serving: 4

Ingredients

- 6 Slices of Bacon, slice In Half
- 12 large Jalapeño
- 8 Ounces of Cream Cheese
- 1 Cup of Grated Cheese
- 2 Tablespoons of Pork & Poultry Rub

Instructions

1. Set the Traeger to 180°F and preheat for fifteen minutes with the lid covered when ready to cook. If Super Smoke is available, use it for the best flavour.

2. Cut the jalapenos longitudinally in half. With a tiny spoon or cutting knife, scrape away any seeds or the ribs. Combine melted cream cheese, that Traeger Pork and Poultry Rub, and shredded cheese in a mixing bowl. Fill each side of a jalapeno with the mixture. Wrap the bacon around the cheese and fasten with the toothpick.

3. Put the jalapenos on the baking sheet with a rim. Put on the grill for thirty minutes to smoke.

4. Raise the grill heat to 375°F and cook for another 30 minutes, or till the bacon gets cooked to your preference. Warm it up and enjoy it!

Grilled Corn on the Cob

Prep Time: 15 Minutes

Cook Time: 30 Minutes

Serving: 6

Ingredients

- 8 medium Ears Fresh Corn
- Some Traeger Veggie Rub
- Some Olive Oil
- Grounded Pepper
- Pinch of Salt
- Salted Butter

Instructions

1. Set the Traeger to 400°F and heat for fifteen minutes with the lid covered when set to cook.

2. Pull the silk from the corn husks by peeling them back. Toss corn with the Traeger Veggie Seasoning and olive oil. Rub, season with salt and black pepper.

3. Put the husks on that grill grate and close. Cook, stirring periodically, for 30 to 35 minutes, or till corn is soft. Serve immediately with butter. Cheers!

Baked Sweet Potatoes

Prep Time: 15 Minutes

Cook Time: 1 Hour

Serving: 8

Ingredients

- 1/4 Cup of Pure Maple Syrup
- 1 Cup of Butter, Softened
- 1/2 Teaspoon of Ground Cinnamon
- 8 large Sweet Potatoes

Instructions

1. To prepare the Maple-Cinnamon Butter, follow these steps: Whisk the butter, some maple syrup, and the cinnamon together in a mixing basin using a wooden spoon. (Conversely, one may use a hand mixer or even a stand mixer to combine the Ingredients.)

2. Place in a medium bowl, cover, and refrigerate until ready to serve.

3. Adjust the Traeger to 375°F when set to cook, place all sweet potatoes on that grill grates, and simmer until tender, about 1 to 1-2 hours based on the size of these potatoes.

4. Cut the slit in the sides of each and inflate the ends with a gentle press.

5. With some Maple-Cinnamon Butter, serve immediately. Cheers!

Roasted Sweet Potato Steak Fries

Prep Time: 10 Minutes

Cook Time: 40 Minutes

Serving: 4

Ingredients

- 3 large Sweet Potatoes

- Pinch of Salt and Pepper

- 4 Tablespoons of Extra-Virgin Olive Oil

- 2 Tablespoons of Fresh diced Rosemary

Instructions

1. Set the Traeger to 460°F and heat for fifteen minutes with the lid covered when set to cook.

2. Sauté sweet potatoes with some olive oil, salt, black pepper, and rosemary before serving.

3. Place on the baking sheet coated with parchment paper and grill. Sauté for fifteen minutes, turn and cook for another 40 to 50 minutes, or until golden and cooked thoroughly.

4. End up serving with the dipping sauce of your choice. Dig!

Bacon-Wrapped Corn on the Cob

Prep Time: 10 Minutes

Cook Time: 20 Minutes

Serving: 4

Ingredients

- 8 Slices of Bacon
- 4 medium Ears Corn
- 1 teaspoon of Chili Powder
- 1 Teaspoon of Freshly Grounded Black Pepper
- Grated Parmesan Cheese

Instructions

1. Take off the silk strings from the corn husks and wash the corn with cold water.

2. Using toothpicks, secure two slices of bacon over each ear of the corn.

3. Some chilli powder and ground black pepper should be sprinkled over each ear of the corn.

4. Heat the grill to 450 degrees F for five to ten minutes with the lid covered.

5. Put the corn ears straight on that Traeger and simmer for about 10 mins, or when the bacon becomes crisp.

Baked Kale Chips

Prep Time: 5 Minutes

Cook Time: 20 Minutes

Serving: 4

Ingredients

- 2 Bunches of Kale, Leaves rinsed And Stalks Removed
- Extra-Virgin Olive Oil
- Some Sea Salt

Instructions

1. Clean the kale leaves properly before placing them on the sheet tray. Spray with some olive oil and season with salt and pepper.

2. When preparing to cook, heat that grill to 250°F with the lid covered for fifteen minutes.

3. Put the sheet tray straight on that grill grates and cook for twenty minutes, or when the kale is gently browned and crunchy. Enjoy!

Beef recipes

Whole Hamburger Buns

Prep Time: 15 Minutes

Cook Time: 25 Minutes

Serving: 5

Ingredients

- 1 medium Tomato, Sliced
- 1 medium White Onion, diced, For Serving
- Some Butter Lettuce, to Serve
- Special Sauce
- Pickle slices, For Serving
- 2 Tablespoons of Mayonnaise
- 2 Teaspoons of Sweet Pickle Relish
- 1 Tablespoon of Ketchup
- 1/2 Teaspoon of Sugar
- 1/2 Teaspoon of White Vinegar

Instructions

1. Form the meat batter into 12-ounce patties. The Traeger Beef Rub should be liberally applied to both sides.

2. For that Special Sauce, combine all sauce Ingredients and keep until set for use.

3. Set the Traeger to 400°F and heat for fifteen minutes with the lid covered when prepared to cook.

4. Place patties on warm grill grates and grill for four minutes

before flipping and cooking for another two minutes.

5. Cook for a further 2 minutes or until the cheese has dissolved.

6. Put the buns on that warm grill to sear if necessary in the last hour of cooking.

7. Take off everything from the barbecue and assemble burgers on the bread with secret sauce, three burger patties, fresh tomato, some lettuce, sliced onions, and pickles. Dig!

Grilled Bacon-Wrapped Hot Dogs

Prep Time: 15 Minutes

Cook Time: 20 Minutes

Serving: 8

Ingredients

- 10 Hot Dog Buns
- 10 Ounce Colby and Tim Monterey Jack Cheese
- 14 Whole Hot Dogs
- 14 Slices of Bacon

Instructions

1. Cut the hot dogs crosswise, exposing a "hinge" solely on a single side, then stuff each with a slice of the cheese.

2. Wrap a piece of bacon on each hot dog in the form of a spiral and fasten with toothpicks.

3. Heat the Traeger to 350°F for fifteen minutes with the lid covered when prepared to cook.

4. Cook these bacon-coated hot dogs on a warm grill grate for 15 to 20 minutes, or when the cheese has completely melted as well as the bacon has caramelized up.

5. Serve instantaneously with the preferred condiments on top of the buns. Relish!

Chorizo Cheese Stuffed Burgers

Prep Time: 20 Minutes

Cook Time: 45 Minutes

Serving: 2

Ingredients

- 4 Ounces of Traeger Rib Rub
- 2 Pounds of Ground Beef
- 10 Ounce of Chorizo
- 4 Whole Burger Buns
- 2 Slices of Cheddar Cheese
- Sliced Tomatoes
- Sliced Lettuce
- Sliced Red Onion

Instructions

1. In a large bowl, combine 2 pounds of the 70/30 ground beef with the Traeger Rib Rub.

2. Make eight 1/4-pound patties out of the ground beef. Prepare the basis of one burger by laying down 1/5 of the cheese slice, 4 oz. Chorizo, with some 1/4 cheese slice. To bind the two patties firmly, place another patty on the top and squeeze the edges around the entire burger.

3. Continue until all four patties are cooked.

4. Preheat the oven to 375 degrees F and leave the lid covered for five to ten minutes when prepared to cook.

5. Cook the burgers for 15-20 minutes on either side of that Traeger. Top every burger with a piece of Cheddar cheese and melt it if preferred. Remove from the Traeger and cover with

foil to rest for ten minutes.

6. Coat the brioche buns with melted butter and grill for 30-35 minutes on the grills while the burgers sit.

7. Remove the buns from the grill and put the burger together with the toppings. Enjoy!

Sweetheart Steak

Prep Time: 5 Minutes

Cook Time: 12 Minutes

Serving: 2

Ingredients

- 1 Teaspoons of Pure Kosher Salt
- 1 Boneless Strip of Steak or Rib Steak
- 2 Teaspoons of Freshly Black Pepper
- 2 Tablespoons of Extra-Virgin Olive Oil
- 2 Tablespoons of Finely Chopped Dark Chocolate

Instructions

1. On the piece of cardboard, draw a big heart in the shape of the meat one wants to use. Construct a heart form out of cardboard, subsequently trim the meat into a heart shape.

2. On the sliced steak, combine all of the Ingredients.

3. Adjust the Traeger to 400°F and heat for fifteen minutes with the lid covered when ready to cook.

4. Grill the steak for 5 - 6 minutes on either side or till it's done. Remove the grill from the heat. Allow for a 5-minute rest period. Enjoy!

Smoked Porterhouse Steak

Prep Time: 15 Minutes

Cook Time: 45 Minutes

Serving: 2

Ingredients

- 2 Tablespoons of Worcestershire Sauce
- 4 Tablespoons of Butter, Melted
- 2 Teaspoons of Dijon Mustard
- 40 Ounces of Steak, Porterhouse
- 1 Teaspoon of Traeger Coffee Rub

Instructions

1. When ready to cook, Preheat the grill to 180°F with the lid covered for 15 minutes.

2. Whisk together the butter, some Worcestershire sauce, and a little mustard till combined. Traeger Coffee Rub should be used on all sides of the steak.

3. Grill the steaks approximately 30 minutes after placing them on the grill grates.

4. Raise the temperature to maximum and preheat the oven. If possible, raise the temperature to 500°F for best results. Once more, lightly brush these steaks with the butter sauce mixture.

5. Place the steaks onto the grill grates after the grill has reached the appropriate temperature. Allow 5 minutes for the steaks to rest before presenting. Enjoy!

Smoked Burgers

Prep Time: 15 Minutes

Cook Time: 2 Hours

Serving: 8

Ingredients

- 1 Pounds of Ground Beef
- 2 Tablespoons of Traeger Beef Rub
- 1 Tablespoon of Worcestershire Sauce

Instruction

1. Combine ground beef, some Worcestershire sauce, and Beef Rub in a mixing bowl.

2. Make eight hamburger patties using the beef mix.

3. Set the Traeger to 180°F and heat for fifteen minutes with the lid covered when ready to cook. If Super Smoke is available, use it for the best flavour.

4. Grill for 2 hours by placing patties straight on the grill grates.

5. Take off from the grill after two hours and serve with one preferred topping. Enjoy!

Chef's Brisket

Prep Time: 10 Minutes

Cook Time: 8 Hours

Serving: 8

Ingredients

- 1 Whole Packer of Beef Brisket
- 1/3 Cup of Kosher Sea Salt
- 2 Tablespoons of Garlic Paste
- 2 Tablespoons of Onion Powder
- 1/3 Cup of Black Pepper

Instructions

1. In a medium bowl, combine the salt, garlic, some onion powder, and ground pepper. Rub the meat well with salt and pepper.

2. When prepared to cook, preheat the Traeger to 225°F with the lid covered for 15 minutes.

3. Put the brisket fat face down on the grill grates in the grill's middle. Smoke the brisket for five hours.

4. Wrap the brisket in butcher paper or any foil after removing it from the grill. Continue to smoke the brisket at 225°F until it achieves an inner temperature of 203°F.

5. Wait for one hour to remove the butcher paper or any foil-covered brisket from the barbeque.

6. Cut the brisket and dish it out once it has rested.

Grilled Wagyu Burgers

Prep Time: 5 Minutes

Cook Time: 8 Minutes

Serving: 4

Ingredients

- 1 Pound of Wagyu Ground Beef
- 6 Slices of American cheese
- Salt and Black Pepper
- 6 fresh Burger Buns
- 1 Sliced Tomato
- Some Butter Lettuce
- 1 Sliced Red Onion

Instructions

1. Set the Traeger to 400°F when prepared to cook.
2. Sprinkle six burger patties generously with salt and black pepper.
3. Put burger patties immediately on the grill grates and cook for four minutes once the grill is heated.
4. Cook for another 4 minutes on the other side, then top with the cheese over the last hour of cooking.
5. Remove off the grill and set aside for 2 minutes to cool.
6. Fresh Butter lettuce, tomato, red onion, and any chosen sauces can be added in the burger. Enjoy!

BBQ Brisket Hot Dog

Prep Time: 5 Minutes

Cook Time: 10 Minutes

Serving: 4

Ingredients

- 6 Whole Hot Dogs
- 1/2 Cup of Heat & Sweet BBQ Sauce
- 1/2 Pound of Leftover Beef Brisket
- 6 fresh Hot Dog Buns
- 1 medium Onion, Diced
- 1/2 Cup of Shredded Cheddar Cheese
- 2 full Jalapeño, Seeded and chopped

Instructions

1. When prepared to cook, Preheat the oven to 440 degrees F and bake for 10-fifteen minutes with the lid covered.

2. Put hot dogs straight on the grill grates and cook for 7-10 minutes, or until hot through and golden brown, flipping periodically.

3. To keep the brisket slices fresh, wrap them in aluminium foil with a little BBQ sauce. Put next to these hot dogs on the warm grill grate and grill until heated through, approximately 4-8 minutes.

4. Put the hot dog on the warmed bun and top with some brisket, extra BBQ sauce, fresh cheddar, sliced onion, and jalapenos to garnish. Enjoy!

Grass-fed Beef Burgers

Prep Time: 10 Minutes

Cook Time: 30 Minutes

Serving: 4

Ingredients

- 1 Pounds of Grass-Fed Ground Beef
- 4 Slices of Provolone Cheese
- 4 Teaspoons of Kosher Salt
- 4 fresh Brioche Burger Buns Burger
- Toppings of the Choice
- 4 Slices of Tomato

Instructions

1. Cut the ground meat into four equal pieces. Take off the meat from the box and form it into the burger patties approximately 5 inches wide. The meat should not be kneaded.

2. When prepared to cook, set Traeger to 425°F and heat it and seal the lid for fifteen minutes.

3. On a grill grate, place the hamburgers. For moderate, cook for twelve minutes. The outside of the meat should be well browned. The thermometer should read 130°F when inserted into the center of the burger.

4. Place provolone slices into the burgers over the last few cooking moments and sear the buns upon this grill. Serve with a side of condiments. Enjoy!

Grilled Tomahawk Steak

Prep Time: 5 Minutes

Cook Time: 1 Hour

Serving: 4

Ingredients

- 2 Tablespoons of Kosher Salt
- 2 medium Tomahawk Steaks
- 2 Tablespoons of Ground Black Pepper
- 1/2 Tablespoon Garlic Powder
- 1 Tablespoon of Paprika
- 1/2 Tablespoon of Onion Powder
- 1 Teaspoon of Ground Mustard
- 1/2 Tablespoon of Brown Sugar
- 1/4 Teaspoon of Cayenne Pepper

Instructions

1. Mix all rub components in a small mixing dish. Coat the steaks all over with the spice.
2. Set the Traeger to 225°F when ready to cook.
3. Put the steaks straight on the grill grates and let them smoke for 50 to 1 hour.
4. Retrieve the steaks from that grill and place them on a cutting board to rest.
5. Preheat the grill to 450 degrees Fahrenheit.
6. Grill the steak for 10 to 15 minutes per side firmly on the grill grates.

7. Remove the steaks from the grill and set them aside to rest for
    five minutes before dishing. Enjoy!

Beginner's Smoked Beef Brisket

Prep Time: 15 Minutes

Cook Time: 12 Hours

Serving: 4

Ingredients

- 1 Flat Cut of Brisket
- 2 Tablespoons of Worcestershire Sauce
- 2 Cups of Beef Broth
- Traeger Beef Rub
- 1/4 Cup of Apple Cider Vinegar Texas BBQ Sauce

Instructions

1. Set the Traeger to 180°F when ready to grill.
2. The Beef Rub should be used on all sides of the beef.
3. To make homemade mop sauce, follow these steps: Mix all beef broth, some beer or cola, some apple cider vinegar, and the Worcestershire sauce inside a sterile spray bottle.
4. Place perhaps the brisket fat-side downwards on the barbecue grate and barbecue for 3 to 5 hours, sprinkling each hour with some mop sauce.
5. Raise the temperature of the grill to 225°F and keep cooking for another 6 to 9 hours.
6. Allow the meat to rest for 20 minutes after foiling it. Using a sharp knife, cut the onion. Serve with a side of BBQ sauce. Cheers!

BBQ Beef Short Ribs

Prep Time: 15 Minutes

Cook Time: 10 Hours

Serving: 8

Ingredients

- 4 Beef Rib Racks
- 1 Cup of Apple Juice
- 1/2 Cup of Beef Rub

Instructions

1. Traeger Beef Rub should be used on all sides of the ribs. Set the Traeger to 225°F when ready to grill.

2. Place these ribs bone-side downwards on the grill grates.

3. Grill for 8 to 12 hours, wiping every 60 minutes with the apple juice. Serve warm after slicing between the ribs. Enjoy!

Grilled Steak

Prep Time: 5 Minutes

Cook Time: 15 Minutes

Serving: 2

Ingredients

- Traeger Rib Rub

- 2 fresh Steaks

Instructions

1. Traeger Rib Rub should be used on all sides of the steaks. Preheat the Traeger to 425°F when ready to start.

2. Place the steak on the grill and grill until it reaches the desired internal temperature. Enjoy!

Smoked Midnight Brisket

Prep Time: 15 Minutes

Cook Time: 12 Hours

Serving: 6

Ingredients

- 1 Tablespoon of Worcestershire Sauce
- 1 Teaspoon of Traeger Chicken Rub
- 1 Tablespoon of Traeger Beef Rub
- 1 Teaspoon of Blackened Rub
- 1 Cup of Beef Broth
- 1 Flat Cut Brisket

Instructions

1. In a mixing dish, combine the Worcestershire sauce and some Traeger rubs. Incorporate the marinade into the meat.

2. Set the Traeger to 180°F when ready to grill.

3. Put the brisket just on a warm grill for 5 to 8 hours.

4. Remove off the grill, triple wrap in foil, and add 1/3 cup of beef broth to 1 cup of beef broth before returning to the grill.

5. Raise the temperature of the grill to 225°F and cook the brisket for another 4 to 6 hours.

6. Remove the steaks from that grill. Serve with the Traeger BBQ sauce of one's choice. Enjoy!

Smoked Pot Roast

Prep Time: 15 Minutes

Cook Time: 6 Hours

Serving: 4

Ingredients

Roast

- 1 fresh Chuck of Roast
- 1 teaspoon of Garlic Powder
- 1 teaspoon of Kosher Salt
- 1 teaspoon of Onion Powder
- 1 teaspoon of Black Pepper

Braise

- 2 Cups of Red Bliss Potatoes, sliced half 2 Cups of Pearl Onions, diced
- 2 Cups of Carrots, Cut Into 3 Inch Slices
- 1 Teaspoon of Ancho Chile Powder 1 Tablespoon of Fresh Rosemary
- 1 Cup of Sherry or Red Wine 1 Tablespoon of Fresh Thyme 2 cups of Beef Stock
- 2 pieces of Dried Chipotle Pepper

Instructions

1. Mix the fresh garlic, onion, kosher salt, and ground pepper in a mixing bowl. Rub the mixture all over the roast.

2. Set the Traeger to 180°F when ready to grill.

3. For 2 hours, grill the chuck roast. Lift the roast off the grill and raise the temperature to 285 degrees Fahrenheit.

4. In a wide Dutch oven, combine that smoked chuck roast, new potatoes, baby carrots, red onions, some ancho Chile powder, white wine, rosemary, fresh thyme, chipotle peppers, and new stock.

5. Put that Dutch oven inside the Traeger with the cover on. Caramelize the roast for three and a half hours at 275°F, or until extremely tender.

6. End up serving with roasted veggies of the choice of potato salad. Enjoy!

Smoked Beef Back Ribs

Prep Time: 15 Minutes

Cook Time: 8 Hours

Serving: 6

Ingredients

- 1/2 Cup of Traeger Beef Rub
- 2 Racks of Beef Back Ribs

Instructions

1. Traeger Beef Rub should be used on either side of the ribs. Set the Traeger to 275°F when ready to grill.

2. Place the ribs bone face down on the warm grill grate. Allow 8-12 hours for cooking.

3. Remove the ribs from the grill and set aside for 30 minutes to rest before cutting and dishing it out. Enjoy!

Smoked Longhorn Brisket

Prep Time: 10 Minutes

Cook Time: 7 Hours

Serving: 8

Ingredients

- 1 Whole Packer Brisket

- 1/4 Cup of Traeger Rib Rub

- 2 Tablespoons of Coffee Grounds

Instructions

1. Preheat Traeger to 250°F when ready to grill.

2. Using Traeger Rib Rub and some coffee grounds, rub the brisket.

3. Put the brisket fat-side downwards on the grill grates and smoke it for 4 to 5 hours.

4. Pull the brisket off the grill and cover it in foil twice. Return the covered brisket to the grill to finish cooking, which should take about 3 to 4 hours.

5. Retrieve from grill and unroll when done. Serve by slicing against the board. Enjoy!

Traeger Filet Mignon

Prep Time: 5 Minutes

Cook Time: 10 Minutes

Serves: 2 people

Ingredients

- 1 fresh Filet Mignon Steaks
- 1 teaspoon of Salt
- 2 cloves of Garlic, Minced
- 1 Teaspoon of Pepper
- 3 Tablespoons of Butter, Softened

Instructions

1. Mix salt, ground pepper, garlic, and melted butter in a medium bowl.
2. Rub the fillets on each side. Allow 10 minutes to rest.
3. Preheat the Traeger to 460°F when ready to grill.
4. Grill the steak for 4 - 6 minutes on every side straight on the barbecue. Enjoy!

Sweet Shrimp & Spicy Sausage Skewers

Prep Time: 30 Minutes

Cook Time: 10 Minutes

Serving: 6

Ingredients

- 24 fresh Shrimp, Peeled and Deveined
- 8 pieces of Italian Pork Sausage
- 1 teaspoon of Dijon Mustard
- 1/2 Cup of Apple Cider Vinegar
- 1 teaspoon of Onion Powder
- 3 Tablespoons of Honey
- 2 cloves of Garlic, Minced
- 1/4 Cup of Canola Oil
- Salt and Black Pepper
- 1 Teaspoon of Dried Thyme

Instructions

1. The white vinegar, Dijon, onion powder, fresh garlic, raw honey, fresh thyme, kosher salt, ground pepper, and canola oil should all be mixed. Toss in the shrimp and set aside for thirty minutes to marinate.

2. Sausage links should be sliced in half crosswise and then into 3-inch chunks.

3. Adjust the temperature to maximum when ready to grill.

4. On these skewers, alternate the sausage and a shrimp. Put shrimp on the grill and grill for 8-12 minutes, or until done.

5. Remove the steaks from the grill and plate. Enjoy!

Fish and Seafood

Baked Salmon Cakes

Prep Time: 20 Minutes

Cook Time: 30 Minutes

Serving: 4

Ingredients

- 2 fresh Salmon Fillet
- 1/2 medium Onion, Diced
- Salt and Black Pepper
- 1 Stalk of Celery, Diced
- 1 Tablespoon of Dried Dill
- 1 small Red Bell Pepper, Diced
- 1 Teaspoon of Fresh Lemon Zest
- 1/4 Teaspoon of Sea Salt
- 1/2 Teaspoon of Black Pepper
- 1 1/2 Tablespoon of Italian Seasoned Breadcrumbs
- 3 Tablespoon of Olive Oil
- 2 medium Eggs

Instructions

1. Set the Traeger to 235°F when ready to cook.

2. Salt and black pepper all salmon fillets and set them straight on the grill grates. Cook until the inner temperature hits 120 degrees Fahrenheit.

3. In a large mixing basin, break up the chilled salmon fillets

using a fork. Combine the onions, celery and carrots, bell pepper, fresh dill, lime zest, salt, ground pepper, bread crumbs, and raw eggs in a mixing bowl. Mix thoroughly.

4. Make 6 patties out of the salmon mixture, each about 2 inches broad. Heat the grill grate by placing a cast-iron skillet on it.

5. In a hot cast-iron skillet, drizzle olive oil. When the oil is heated, add the patties in batches towards the cast iron skillet. Cook for 12 - 15 minutes, turning halfway through the cooking time. Enjoy!

Cajun Smoked Shrimp

Prep Time: 20 Minutes

Cook Time: 5 Minutes

Serving: 4

Ingredients

Main

- 1/4 Cup of Extra-Virgin Olive Oil

- 2 cloves of Garlic, Minced

- 1 Lime, Juiced

- 1 Tablespoon of Cajun Seasoning

- 2 Pound of Raw Shrimp, washed And Deveined

- 1 teaspoon of Kosher Salt

Instructions

1. Make sure they have enough time to marinate. Combine all the Ingredients in a big sealed plastic bag and carefully toss to coat all shrimp. If necessary, the shrimp could be covered and marinated for 2 - 3 hours.

2. Set the Traeger to 500°F when ready to grill.

3. Skewer that shrimp and set them straight on a heated grill grate. Cook till the meat is opaque, three to four minutes per side. Eat and have fun!

Simple Glazed Salmon Fillets

Prep Time: 5 Minutes

Cook Time: 25 Minutes

Serving: 2

Ingredients

- 4 Center-Cut fresh Salmon Fillets, with skin
- 1/2 Cup of Mayonnaise
- Traeger Feather and fin Rub
- 2 Tablespoons of Dijon Mustard
- 1 Tablespoon of Fresh Chopped Tarragon
- 1 Tablespoon of Fresh Lemon Juice
- Some Lemon Wedges

Instructions

1. The Traeger Feather Rub has been used to flavour the fillets.

2. How to Make the Glaze: In a small mixing dish, mix the mayonnaise and Dijon mustard. Combine the lime juice and dill or the tarragon in a mixing bowl.

3. The glaze should be applied to the meat side of both fillets. Preheat the Traeger to 360°F when ready to cook.

4. Place the salmon fillet's skin surface downwards on the grill grate.

5. Cook for 30 to 35 minutes on the grill.

6. Serve shortly on a dish or plates, garnished with lemon slices and minced dill. Relish!

Smoked Trout

Prep Time: 10 Minutes

Cook Time: 2 Hours

Serving: 6

Ingredients

- 8 Trout Fillets
- 1/4 Cup of Salt
- 1 Gallon of Water
- 1/2 Cup of Brown Sugar
- 2 Tablespoons of Soy Sauce
- 1 Tablespoon of Black Pepper

Instructions

1. Wash and prepare the fresh fish.
2. To make the brine, combine 1 gallon of water, dark brown sugar, some soy sauce, kosher salt, and ground pepper in a mixing bowl and whisk to mix the sugar and salt.
3. Set the Traeger to 225°F when ready to grill.
4. Take the fish out of the brine and wipe them dry. Based on the diameter of a trout, cook it straight on the grill grates for 2 hours. Serve warm or chilled. Enjoy!
5. When the fish becomes opaque and begins to flake, it is cooked. Serve warm or chilled. Enjoy!

Grilled Blackened Saskatchewan Salmon

Prep Time: 15 Minutes

Cook Time: 30 Minutes

Serving: 4

Ingredients

- 2 fresh Salmon Fillets
- Italian Dressing
- Traeger Blackened Rub
- Some Lemon Wedges

Instructions

1. Season the salmon with some Traeger Rub after brushing it with the Italian dressing.

2. Preheat the Traeger to 325°F when prepared to cook.

3. Grill the salmon for 15 to 20 minutes just on the grill, or until it achieves a core temperature of 145°F and flakes readily.

4. Take the fish off the grill. Offer with lemon slices on the side. Enjoy!

Smoked Seafood Ceviche

Prep Time: 20 Minutes

Cook Time: 1 Hour

Serving: 4

Ingredients

- 1 Pound of Sea Scallops, Shucked
- 1 Tablespoon of Canola Oil
- 1 Pound of Shrimp, washed And Deveined
- 1 Lime, Juiced
- 1 medium Orange, Juiced
- 1 medium Lemon Juice
- 1 Pinch of Red Pepper Flakes
- 1 teaspoon of Garlic Powder
- 2 Teaspoons of Salt
- 1 teaspoon of Onion Powder
- 1/2 Teaspoon of Black Pepper
- ½ medium Onion, Diced
- 1 chopped Avocado
- 1 Tablespoon of chopped Cilantro

Instructions

1. Mix the shrimp, all scallops, and canola oil inside a mixing basin. Preheat the grill to 175 degrees F when prepared to cook.

2. Place the shrimp as well as scallops upon this grill for 45 minutes to smoke. Prepare all of the remaining Ingredients and

combine them in a big mixing basin while they are cooking.

3. Bring this grill up to 350 degrees and cook for another 5 minutes once the shrimp and sea scallops are smoked.

4. Allow both scallops and shrimp to cool before cutting them half width-wise and mixing them with the other bowl components. Offer with corn chips on the side.

Teriyaki Salmon

Prep Time: 1 Hour

Cook Time: 10 Minutes

Serving: 2

Ingredients

- 1 Cup of Soy Sauce
- 4 cloves of Garlic
- 6 Tablespoons of Brown Sugar
- 1 Tablespoon of Ginger, Minced
- 2 medium Orange Zest
- 2 medium Orange, Juiced
- 4 Pieces of Salmon Fillets Chopped Scallions
- 1 Tablespoon of Sesame Seeds Sesame Seeds, toasted

Instructions

1. In a skillet, combine everything except the sesame seeds and the fish. Bring to the boil, reduce to low heat and continue to cook until a syrupy viscosity is obtained.
2. Braise for 1 hour with sesame seeds and fish.
3. Bring the sauce to a boil after removing the salmon from the marinade.
4. Bring the grill to hot temperature for 5 to 10 minutes with the lid covered. Put the salmon fillets skinned side up upon this grill grate.
5. Grill the salmon for 3 - 4 minutes per side, brushing it with some Teriyaki Sauce.
6. When the salmon is cooked, remove it out from the pan. Enjoy!

Baked Tuna Noodle Casserole

Prep Time: 30 Minutes

Cook Time: 45 Minutes

Serving: 4

Ingredients

- 1 Wheat Pasta, Box
- 1 Cup of Almond Milk
- 2 cups of Whole Milk Yogurt
- 1 Cup of Grated Jack Cheese
- 1 Teaspoon of Ground Mustard
- 1 Cup of Sliced Button Mushrooms
- 1/2 Teaspoon of Celery Salt
- 10 Ounces of Tuna, Cooked
- 1 Cup of Peas, Canned

Instructions

1. Over hot temperatures, bring a huge pot of seasoned water to a boil.

2. Cook the pasta after adding it.

3. Combine yoghurt, cow's milk, and ground Dijon mustard, and celery salts in a wide mixing bowl. In a large mixing bowl, combine the mushrooms, tuna fish, peas, and drained pasta. Half of the cheese should be folded.

4. Fill a baking dish halfway with the batter and cover with the leftover cheese.

5. Preheat the Traeger to 350°F when ready to grill.

6. Grill for 30 mins with the casserole dish straight on the grill grates. Enjoy!

Baked Whole Fish in Sea Salt

Prep Time: 10 Minutes

Cook Time: 30 Minutes

Serving: 4

Ingredients

- 3 Pound of the Whole Branzino
- 1 Lemon, Thinly Sliced
- 10 Sprig of Thyme Sprigs
- 5 Cup of Sea Salt
- Some Olive Oil
- 10 Egg White
- 1 medium Lemon Juice

Instructions

1. When fully prepared to cook, set the temperature to maximum.

2. The fish's fins should be clipped, and the gills should be removed. Thyme and lime slices should be stuffed into the cavity. Wrap in the kosher salt after whipping this same egg whites with soft peaks.

3. Preheat the oven to 350°F and cook for thirty minutes straight on the grill grate.

4. Detach the fish from either the grill and set it aside for 10 minutes to cool.

5. Peel the skin from the fish and coat it in olive oil with a squeeze of lime. Enjoy!

Honey Balsamic Salmon

Prep Time: 5 Minutes

Cook Time: 25 Minutes

Serving: 2

Ingredients

- 1 Tablespoon of Honey
- 1 large Salmon Fillet
- 1/2 Cup of Balsamic Vinegar
- Traeger Feather and fin Rub
- 1 Tablespoon of Minced Garlic

Instructions

1. Use the Fin & Feather Rub to flavour the fillet.

2. To make the glaze, follow these steps: In a medium bowl, mix the vinegar, garlic, and raw honey. Sauté over moderate flame until the liquid has been reduced by half. Apply the glaze on the fillet with the brush.

3. Preheat the Traeger to 350°F when prepared to cook.

4. Place the salmon piece just on the grill grate and season with salt and pepper. Cook for 20 - 25 minutes on the grill.

5. Quickly transfer to a tray or plates and garnish. Enjoy!

Grilled Fresh Fish

Prep Time: 5 Minutes

Cook Time: 15 Minutes

Serving: 2

Ingredients

- 1 Whole Fillet Of fish
- Traeger Feather and fin Rub
- 2 medium Lemons

Instructions

1. Preheat the Traeger to 325°F when ready to grill.

2. Allow 30 minutes to marinate the fish in Fin & Feather Rub.

3. Straight on the barbecue grates, put the fish and lemon. Cook for ten to fifteen minutes. Take cautious not to overcook the food.

4. Garnish with lemons that have been grilled. Enjoy!

Smoked Salmon Candy

Prep Time: 10 Minutes

Cook Time: 3 Hours

Serving: 4

Ingredients

- 2 Cups of Gin
- 1/2 Cup of Kosher Salt
- 1 Cup of Dark Brown Sugar
- 1 Cup of Maple Syrup
- Some Dark Brown Sugar
- 3 Pounds of Salmon
- 1 Tablespoon of Black Pepper
- 1 cup of Vegetable Oil

Instructions

1. Mix all curative Ingredients in a medium mixing basin. Place the fish in the cure after cutting it into 2-ounce slices. Set the Traeger to 180°F when ready to grill.

2. Vegetable oil should be sprayed on the foil. Place the salmon onto foil and top with more brown sugar.

3. The foil is placed immediately upon this grill grate. Grill the fish for 2 - 3 hours with the lid closed.

4. Serve warm or cold. Enjoy!

Smoky Crab Dip

Prep Time: 5 Minutes

Cook Time: 20 Minutes

Serving: 6

Ingredients

- 1/3 Cup of Mayonnaise
- 1 teaspoon of Smoked Paprika
- Some Butter Crackers
- 3 Ounces of Sour Cream
- 1/4 Teaspoon of Cayenne Pepper
- Salt and Black Pepper
- 1 1/2 Pound of Lump Crab Meat
- Chopped Scallions

Instructions

1. Set the Traeger and adjust the flame to 325 degrees when ready to grill.

2. Meanwhile, in a big mixing bowl, carefully combine all of the Ingredients, excluding the crackers, topping scallions, and the crab meat, in a large mixing bowl. Then add crab meat.

3. Season with salt and pepper to taste, then transfer to the oven-safe baking tray.

4. Preheat oven to 200°F and bake for 20–25 minutes. Add more diced scallions as a garnish. Relish!

Seared Bluefin Tuna Steaks

Prep Time: 5 Minutes

Cook Time: 5 Minutes

Serving: 2

Ingredients

- 2 medium Tuna, Steak Some Sriracha
- Salt and Black Pepper
- Some Olive Oil
- 1 cup of Soy Sauce

Instructions

1. Brush both sides of the tuna steaks with olive oil and season with kosher salt and ground black pepper.

2. Turn the heat up to high when ready to cook. Grill tuna steaks for 3 minutes on all sides.

3. Take the tuna off the grill.

4. Serve with some Soy Sauce and the Sriracha sauce combination. Enjoy!"

Grilled Crab Legs with Herb Butter

Prep Time: 15 Minutes

Cook Time: 15 Minutes

Serving: 2

Ingredients

- 12 Tablespoons of Butter
- 4 Pounds of King Crab Legs
- 3 Tablespoons of chopped Fresh Herbs
- 3 medium Lemons, Cut into Slices

Instructions

1. Preheat the Traeger to 375°F when ready to grill.

2. In a large stainless-steel saucepan, combine the butter, fresh garlic, dried herbs, and a sprinkle of salt. To melt the cheese, place it on the grill for five minutes.

3. Cut the crab legs down the centre and spread herb butter on the flesh, saving a quarter for dishing.

4. Put the crab legs flesh side up over the grill grates. Grill for 5–10 minutes.

5. Crab legs should be served with lime wedges and the herb butter that has been set aside. Enjoy!

Traeger Jerk Shrimp

Prep Time: 15 Minutes

Cook Time: 10 Minutes

Serving: 8

Ingredients

- 1 Tablespoon of Brown Sugar
- 1 teaspoon of Garlic Powder
- 1 Tablespoon of Smoked Paprika
- 1/4 Teaspoon of Thyme, Ground
- 1 teaspoon of Sea Salt
- 1/4 Teaspoon of Ground Cayenne Pepper
- 1 Lemon Zest
- 3 Tablespoons of Olive Oil
- 2 Pounds of Shrimp in Shell

Instructions

1. In a medium mixing dish, combine the spices, kosher salt, and lemon zest. Put the shrimp in the large baking bowl, sprinkle olive oil, and season with the spice combination.

2. Preheat the oven to 470°F when ready to grill.

3. Grill the shrimp for 1–2 minutes on each side on the grills.

4. Lemon wedges, fresh parsley, fresh mint, and some Caribbean Hot Sauce are served on the side. Enjoy!

Whole Vermillion Red Snapper

Prep Time: 5 Minutes

Cook Time: 20 Minutes

Serving: 6

Ingredients

- 1 medium Vermilion Red Snapper
- 1 Whole sliced Lemon
- 4 cloves of Garlic, Chopped
- 2 Sprigs of Rosemary Sprigs
- Sea Salt and Fresh Grounded Black Pepper

Instructions

1. Set the temperature to maximum when ready to grill.
2. Garlic should be stuffed into the inner side of the fish. Season the fish with a pinch of salt, ground pepper, rosemary, and lime juice.
3. Fish is cooked straight on the grill grate. Simmer for twenty minutes to 25 minutes. End up serving. Enjoy!

Grilled Clams in Garlic Butter

Prep Time: 10 Minutes

Cook Time: 8 Minutes

Serving: 6

Ingredients

- 24 Clams of Littleneck

- 3 cloves of Garlic, Minced

- 8 Tablespoons of Butter

- 2 Tablespoons of Parsley, Minced

- 6 Lemons, cut in Wedges

- 2 Teaspoons of Pernod Liqueur

Instructions

1. Start the Traeger and adjust the flame to 500 degrees Fahrenheit when ready to cook.

2. In a thermally stable pan, combine the butter, fresh garlic, parsley, and the juice of 2 lime wedges.

3. Grill these clams for 5 - 10 minutes, straight on the grill grates.

4. Gently move these opened clams to a pan with melted butter using tongs.

5. Garnish with the leftover lime wedges in a deep serving dish with all clams and butter.

Desserts

Mangoes Grilled with Lime & Coconut

Prep Time: 10 Minutes

Cook Time: 15 Minutes

Serves: 2 people

Ingredients

- 2 Tablespoons of Maple Syrup
- 4 Mangoes Whole Ripe
- 3 Cup of Coconut Yogurt
- 1 Cup of Coconut Flakes
- 1 Teaspoon of Chile Powder
- 3 Tablespoons of Lime Zest

Instructions

1. Set the Traeger to 500°F & preheat for fifteen min with the lid covered when you're ready to cook.

2. Mangoes are peeled and sliced into cheeks, then brushed with maple syrup.

3. On the Traeger grill, cook the mango until golden brown. Fry the coconut flakes in a pan on the grill until they are light golden brown.

4. Combine the coconut yogurt, toasted coconut flakes, mango cheeks, fresh lime zest, & chili powder. Enjoy.

Seasonal Fruit Grilled with Gelato

Prep Time: 5 Minutes

Cook Time: 5 Minutes

Serves: 2 people

Ingredients

- 3 Tablespoons of Turbinado Sugar
- 2 Whole Peaches, Apricots or Plums Gelato, For Serving
- 1/4 Cup of Honey

Instructions

1. Set the Traeger to 450°F & preheat for fifteen min with the lid covered when you're ready to cook.

2. Remove the pit from each piece of fruit before slicing it in half. Brush honey on the cut side & sprinkle sugar on top.

3. Place the fruit straight on the grill, with cut-side down, till grill marks appear.

4. Remove the fruits from the grill & serve with scoops of gelato. If desired, drizzle with honey. Enjoy.

Smoked Cold Cheese

Prep Time: 5 Minutes

Cook Time: 2 Hours

Serves: 8 people

Ingredients

- Mozzarella, cheddar, or provolone cheese

Instructions

1. When you're ready to cook, preheat the Traeger to 165°F & shut the lid for fifteen minutes.

2. Place a half-size baking pan in the middle of a full-size baking pan. Fill the half-size pan with ice until it reaches the top.

3. Place the cheese in a half-size pan on top of a cooling rack or toothpicks to enable air to circulate the cheese & prevent it from sticking. Place the pan on the grill to cook.

4. One hour of smoked cheese flips the cheese over on the grill. Continue to smoke for another hour after adding additional ice to the melting water surrounding the pan.

5. Wrap the cheese in parchment paper and remove it from the grill. Refrigerate for two to three days to enable flavours to meld. The smoke taste will be mellowed as a result of this.

6. Remove from the fridge two to three days later, unwrap, slice, & serve with your favourite cracker, pickled veggies, & wine. Enjoy.

Caramel Pecan Brownie in the Oven

Prep Time: 15 Minutes

Cook Time: 50 Minutes

Serves: 6 people

Ingredients

- 1/4 Cup of Butter
- 3/4 Cup of Pecans, Halves
- 1½ Cup of Brown Sugar
- 1 Cup of All-Purpose Flour
- 3/4 Cup of Heavy Cream
- 1/2 Cup of Cocoa Powder
- 1/2 Teaspoon of Salt
- 3/4 Teaspoon of Baking Soda
- 6 Tablespoon of Melted Butter
- 6 Ounce of Chopped Chocolate
- 3 Eggs, Large

Instructions

1. To make the Pecan-Caramel Sauce, roast the nuts in a 9-inch cast- iron skillet over medium flame. Pecans should be toasted for five minutes, stirring periodically. Toss the nuts with 1/4 cup butter & 1/2 cup brown sugar. Stir until the brown sugar and butter have melted and mixed.

2. Remove the pecans from the heat and slowly pour in 1/2 cup of heavy cream. Return to the heat and whisk until all of the creams are mixed. Remove the pan from the heat and put it aside.

3. Whisk together the brown sugar, cocoa powder, flour, baking

soda, & salt in a large mixing bowl to make the brownies. Mix in the melted butter, eggs, & cream well. Fold in the milk chocolate chunks. Over the caramel pecan mixture, pour the brownie batter.

4. Preheat the Traeger to 325°F for 15 minutes with the lid closed when ready to cook. Cook the brownies in the Traeger for 35-40 mins, or until a toothpick inserted in the middle comes out clean.

5. Put the cast iron pan on the grill grate & cook for 35-40 mins, or until a toothpick inserted in the middle comes out clean.

6. Allow cooling for at least ten minutes after removing from the grill. Serve with ice cream while it's still warm. Enjoy.

Bacon-Salted Caramel Dark Chocolate Brownies

Prep Time: 10 Minutes

Cook Time: 40 Minutes

Serves: 8 people

Ingredients

- 1/2 Cup of Kosher Salt
- 8 Strips of Bacon
- 1 Jar of Caramel Sauce
- 1 Whole Brownie Mix

Instructions

1. Cook a few bacon pieces (6 - 8) until extremely crisp for the bacon salt: It should take approximately 25 mins at 350 degrees. Allow cooling before pulsing until finely minced in a food processor. Combine 1/2 cup kosher salt in a mixing bowl. Keep it refrigerated until you're ready to use it.

2. Preheat the oven to 350 ° F. & leave the lid covered for 10 to 15 mins when ready to cook.

3. Follow the box Instructions for making the brownies & pour them onto a prepared pan. Using around two tbsp. Of the caramel sauce, drizzle it over the brownie batter. Add about 1 tsp of bacon salt to the mixture. Place immediately on the preheated Traeger grill grate.

4. Bake the brownies for about 20-25 mins, or until the batter begins to firm up. Remove from the grill & top with 2 tbsp. Additional caramel sauce & a pinch of bacon salt. Return the brownies to the grill for another 20-25 mins, till a toothpick pierced in the centre comes out clean.

5. If you want a little more caramel, pour another layer on the

warm brownies and finish with a pinch of bacon salt. Allow for full cooling before cutting the brownies into squares. To keep the brownies from clinging to the knife, clean it between each slice. Enjoy.

S'mores Croissants on the Grill

Prep Time: 15 Minutes

Cook Time: 2 Minutes

Serves: 6 people

Ingredients

- 6 Croissants

- 8 Ounce of Chocolate

- 25 Large Regular Marshmallows

Instructions

1. When ready to cook, preheat the grill on high for 15 minutes with the lid covered.

2. Place them cut-side down croissant halves on the grate of the grill and toast the croissants for approximately 1 minute. (They will rapidly toast, so keep an eye on them.)

3. Remove the s'mores from the grill & stack with marshmallows & chocolate pieces before topping with the other half of the croissant to create a toasted croissant s'mores sandwich.

4. Put the croissant sandwiches on a grill for 30 secs to 1 min to melt the chocolate & toast the marshmallows.

5. Retrieve the s'mores from the grill & serve while it is still hot & gooey. Enjoy.

Baked Caramelized Bourbon Pears

Prep Time: 10 Minutes

Cook Time: 30 Minutes

Serves: 4 people

Ingredients

- 1/4 Cup of Brown Sugar

- 3 Whole Sliced Ripe Pears

- 1/4 Cup of Bourbon

- 1 teaspoon of Vanilla Extract

- 2 Tablespoons of Butter, Melted

- 1/2 Teaspoon of Salt

Instructions

1. Preheat the oven to 325°F with the lid covered for fifteen minutes when ready to cook.

2. Pears should be peeled and cored. Arrange them in a baking dish that has been greased.

3. Mix the brown sugar, butter, bourbon, vanilla, cinnamon, & salt in a small bowl. Over the pears, pour the bourbon mixture.

4. Put the baking dish on the grill grate, cover the lid, and bake the pears for 30-35 mins, or until fork-tender.

5. Place the pears on a serving dish and drizzle the caramelized bourbon mixture over them.

6. Over vanilla ice cream, serve warm. Enjoy.

Whipped Smoked Cream

Prep Time: 7 Hours

Cook Time: 40 Minutes

Serves: 4 people

Ingredients

- 1/2 Cup of Sour Cream
- 3 Cup of Heavy Cream
- 1/2 Tablespoon of Vanilla Extract
- 6 Tablespoons of Powdered Sugar

Instructions

1. Set the temperature to 180°F & preheat for fifteen min with the lid covered when ready to cook.

2. In an oven-safe pan or dish, pour the heavy cream. Cast iron should not be used.

3. Place the cream on the Traeger grill & cook for twenty minutes on the Smoke setting. Smoke for 40 mins for a heavier smoke taste.

4. Remove the cream from the Traeger & set it aside to cool for 1 hour. Refrigerate for at least six hours.

5. Pour the whipping cream into the mixing bowl with the rest of the Ingredients. Whisk the cream just until firm peaks form.

6. Serve with fruit or your preferred desserts. Enjoy.

9 788367 110211